Glimpses

Glimpses

By

DECLAN HENRY

THE LONDON PRESS

Glimpses

First published by The London Press, UK 2007

Second Edition 2010

ISBN: 978-1-905006-12-0

A C.I.P reference is available from the British Library.

Dedicated to my dear parents
Kathleen and Pat

Introduction

by

BLUECARE SOCIAL CARE

In *Glimpses*, Declan Henry utilises his artistic talents to bring to centre stage, stories reflective of the challenges being faced on a daily basis by young people from all walks of life.

Bluecare Social Care recruitment agency, who have worked with Declan in recent years, respect the work and contributions made by social workers, especially those who use their talent, skill and personal time to further support and bring recognition to causes and groups which they are passionate about. In this regard, we are pleased to be able to support Declan on the debut of his first book, *Glimpses*.

Glimpses, a collection of short stories, offers a gritty, yet nonetheless realistic, insight into the lives of young people as they struggle to exist in the life and circumstances which they have been dealt. For the most part, these stories are not written with happy endings that might ordinarily leave the reader with a sense of closure – either good or bad. Rather, they depict real life as Declan has observed through his work with young people – and like real life, the ending is unknown. Therefore, the ability to close the book, both literally and figuratively, is much more difficult as these stories weave their way into your psyche and beg the question: *What could, would or can make a difference?*

Declan's collection of short stories will have widespread appeal striking multiple chords across an array of readership. To young people it may be resonant of solidarity and embolden their spirit of survival; to professionals who work with young people it shall no doubt add to the discussion of social, economic and political implications if conditions for youth are left unabated; and, for the general populous, it may galvanise individual consciousness in embracing the mantra that 'one person can make a difference.' Whichever the impact, Declan's work is a contribution worth reading as well as a wake-up call to the realities of far too many youth in our present society.

Bluecare Social Care is the UK's largest provider of Qualified Social Workers; and with innovative recruitment methods, pioneering training and post-placement support, has received recognition for its professionalism, investment and contribution to social work.

Foreword

Three out of every four children enjoy a good enough childhood, and manage to successfully navigate the transition from adolescence to adulthood – emerging as sane and well-adjusted human beings. However, the remaining one in four of our children is ill-treated, abused, brutalised and abandoned through circumstances beyond their control.

The stories contained in *Glimpses* come from the insight and knowledge I have gained while working as a social worker since the 1990's. In my experience, a person does not have to look far these days before they come across teenagers displaying anti-social behaviour in our towns and cities. In certain areas, it would seem to have become reasonably commonplace to witness young people blocking entrances to shops, shouting abuse, smoking cannabis, harassing elderly people and deliberately damaging property.

Hardly a day passes without some headline, article or TV programme highlighting the problem of teenagers getting into trouble with the law as well as a plethora of accounts relating to violent gangs and feral youths causing havoc in their local communities. Other stories refer to an escalating knife culture, drug use and underage sex.

However, the teenagers that you read about in the media or maybe see or hear about in the area where you live are not 'typical' teenagers. They are unlikely to come from happy backgrounds. Generally, they have not been nurtured, cared for, or shown sufficient love and attention. They tend not to have had positive role models to guide them through their formative years or have had parents or carers who will have given them a secure and stable structure consisting of a balance of discipline and love in equal measure. Rather inconsistent boundaries coupled with fear, brutality, abuse and neglect have featured in their lives and as a result this has led them to express increased levels of anger and anti-social behaviour. In light of this it is unfortunate that the media have labelled these children as 'yobs', when they are in fact some of the most vulnerable young people we have in society.

As a social worker I take the view that it is essential for the young people in our society, leading lives like those featured in *Glimpses*, to be given opportunities that will help them re-establish belief in their capabilities and thus assist them to begin rebuilding their shattered lives. These young people really do know the difference between right and wrong, but, because of the trauma they have experienced they have lost connection with the spiritual essence of themselves. Their psyches are so damaged by the life events they have experienced they are inclined to dive headlong into anti-social and criminal behaviour.

Their untapped potential has never been given the opportunity by circumstances to manifest itself and see the light of day. They need a support system in place that will help them rebuild their self-confidence and realise that they can have a better and more meaningful life. Young people often need support settling into an educational provision that is best suited to their needs. Many will benefit from being referred to training provisions where they can learn new skills to enable better access into employment. Social workers need to be able to address contentious and sensitive issues with young people in order to bring about change. This can cover a range of issues that includes anger management, peer pressure, social skills, self-esteem and integrity, problem-solving, the consequences of offending and personal responsibility. Liaising with parents and carers and suggesting mediation or family therapy in terse situations is high on the agenda. Many parents and carers also benefit from attending parenting groups or from having a parenting co-ordinator assigned to them. Some will need counselling from Child and Adolescent Mental Health Services whilst others will need specialist drug and alcohol intervention to curtail addiction. Matching a young person with a mentor who can support and guide them through change is also a valuable option.

The reading of *Glimpses* is not for the faint-hearted. But its underlying message is clear – to outline the myriad reasons why we have so many angry and disaffected young people in today's society and the challenges faced by social workers in bringing about positive change into these broken lives.

I hope the stories in *Glimpses* will stimulate a more profound level of discussion on this important social issue – a discussion that is both realistic and compassionate.

DECLAN HENRY

Aymon

Aymon looked at his mother in a surly and intimidating manner. He hated the way she thought she could lecture him, especially since he thought her behaviour was worse than his. She had asked him to stop smoking cannabis in the house because they were expecting the family social worker to arrive and Aymon's mother knew that she would be able to smell the leftover smoke. His response to his mother was a 'hiss' and a 'V' sign, whilst he remained slumped in his seat with his feet up, happily puffing away.

Aymon liked being the 'boss' at home and thought he automatically earned his position by being the eldest male in the family. He would come and go as he pleased and this meant that his mother seldom had any idea where he was. He was part of a local group of youths who enticed him into offending and drugs. There were times when he didn't return home at all. Aymon's mother used to attempt to challenge him for staying out overnight without telling her, but he usually threw a tantrum when she tried to tell him off. The after-effects of a heavy night of drugs and partying often left him in a cantankerous mood.

Aymon had no respect for his mother. He thought she was lazy and that all she did was watch television and smoke cigarettes. Years of blaming her for him having no father had meant that his relationship with her was often volatile. Recently this had resulted in him being violent towards his mother, which left her with bruising on her face. Aymon resented his mother for informing the social worker about him hitting her during the visit. The social worker pointed out to him that he was developing a nasty temper because of his drug use. Aymon took umbrage to the social worker's comments and gave her a venomous stare before answering.

'That's none of your business,' he replied, before muttering under his breath, 'Fucking bitch.'

Then one day, something absolutely amazing and unexpected happened. Aymon was watching a film when the doorbell rang. He presumed it was one of his friends but when he opened the door he discovered a man who he did not know standing there. The man asked if his mother was in but before Aymon had a chance to reply, the man brushed past him. Aymon felt a little frightened by this sudden action. This soon turned to shock when he listened to the conversation between his mother and the man.

Goose pimples crept all over Aymon when the identity of the stranger became clear. It was his father who had returned. Here, before him, was the person at whom he had directed anger, bitterness and hatred for as long as he could remember. This figure at the back of his mind had become the excuse for his bad behaviour. This was the man who he blamed for his problems and unhappiness, and now, he was in the same room with him. Aymon felt completely dumbfounded by his father's sudden and unexpected presence.

Life changed for Aymon overnight. It transpired that his father had just been released from prison where he had served nearly ten years for murder. Aymon hated the way his father had returned to family life, assuming that he could just pick up the pieces where he left off before his long absence. He didn't consider his father as part of the family. Although he knew that his mother had stopped looking after her appearance and had few friends, he hated the thought of her having sex with this man, his father, who was a stranger to him.

Aymon was no longer the boss at home. A new master had taken up the reins and expected his rules to be adhered to. Although Aymon's father took pride in his hardened image, he liked to adopt a criminal chivalry that prohibited him from hitting women or taking drugs and because of this he directed his anger towards Aymon.

Aymon was stopped from smoking cannabis at home and was told by his father that he was expected to be at home each evening by ten o'clock. He hated these new rules and challenged his father at every opportunity. However, one day Aymon went too far in his obstinacy to the new conditions and for this, his father responded with hard punches. The fact that his mother disclosed, to his father, how he had hit her did not earn Aymon any leniency when he pleaded for him to stop. However, as the weeks went by, he got bored playing the father figure and began to spend less time at home. His control over Aymon lessened as a result.

At this stage, Aymon's relationship with his mother began to change. On the surface it appeared that he had become more caring and protective towards her; he helped with household tasks and spent more time with his siblings.

But a plan had already formed in his mind. He had discussed the situation with his girlfriend, and together, they had hatched a plan to sabotage Aymon's parents' reconciliation. Together they agreed that Aymon should start to sow seeds of doubt in his mother's mind about his father seeing other women. Aymon liked this idea but reckoned that it would be unwise to rush home one evening and blurt out such suspicions. Instead he planned to start telling her things slowly under the pretence that he was genuinely concerned about her getting hurt. Hence, pretending to be a devoted son was part of the scheme.

It started gently with him telling her stories that he had heard about his father from friends and neighbours. There was truth in some of the rumours but Aymon exaggerated and added bits on. His mother was furious when he told her that his father had been seen drinking and gambling in a casino and that he had been seen in the company of prostitutes on several occasions. Aymon knew she believed him and she told him that she was tired of supporting his father financially. His father had refused to get a job but still demanded total control over their social benefits, which left Aymon's mother with little money for food and household bills.

The more information that Aymon fed his mother the more she believed him. When he saw her believing his stories, he started emphasising how well they all had coped when his father was in prison and added how they could manage without him if he were to leave again. Aymon made these assertions with the promise that if this were to happen, he would take his responsibilities at home more seriously than before.

Then one evening, matters came to a head and a violent argument broke out between Aymon's mother and father. They shouted and yelled at each other. Incomprehensible accusations of all kinds were screamed at the top of their voices. Objects flew across the room and the air was filled with the sounds of broken glass and crockery. Fascinated, Aymon and his brothers sat and watched the fighting. Suddenly, Aymon jumped up from his seat and started yelling at his father to stop.

'Stop hitting her, you bastard or else I will kill you,' Aymon threatened.

'Go on then, try it, fucking try it, if you think you're so strong,' his father replied.

Rage swelled Aymon's muscles as he ran to the kitchen to pick up a knife and then, upon returning to the room, he threatened to kill his father if he did not leave the house. Aymon held the knife out and stared directly at his father. His father swore at him and told him that he would 'fix things' with him later as he walked towards the door to leave.

Afterwards Aymon stood with his back to the door, shaking and breathing heavily. He considered his actions to be truly vindicated and for the first time in ages, he began to feel a sense of relief. Little did he realise at this stage that his actions were far from being ideal. The anger and hatred he had towards his father would become so fixed that it would haunt him in the months and years to follow.

Home life, notwithstanding the bitterness he held towards his father, began to return to normal. Aymon resumed his old habits and ceased playing the role of concerned son. The fixation he held previously about being an abandoned child was now replaced with a vengeful hatred towards his father. He fully demonstrated this anytime he met him in public.

'Aren't you back in the nick yet? – you useless bastard!' he would often shout at his father. 'Best place for you,' he would then add.

What hadn't changed though was the dreary life that Aymon lived at home. In fact, it had now worsened; his behaviour became even more challenging towards his mother. He announced to her one day that he had asked his girlfriend to move in with him. Cannabis was again smoked in the house, he refused to attend school and the days were spent either sleeping or being in a foul mood. He often committed street robberies without a trace of remorse and never feared getting caught. The saddest thing of all was perhaps that there was no one influential enough in his life to get him to stop. Daily misery continued in every aspect of his life but Aymon didn't realise this. He felt happy and contented with his routine and anyone who tried to contradict him was met with a cocksure reply. Indeed, Aymon always appeared to have sarcastic answers ready and waiting at his disposal.

Brad

Brad lived in a large residential area with his mother and siblings. Brad had lived in this place all his life and was oblivious to the greyness and depressing feel the area exhibited. He frequently played truant from school, which allowed him plenty of time to discover otherwise hidden nooks and crannies, in the vast sprawl of streets and alleys that made up his immediate neighbourhood.

On the surface, Brad looked every bit the average teenager. He wore the same style of clothes all year round: his attire consisted of tracksuit bottoms, trainers and a hooded top – pulled constantly up over his head. Brad also sported a gold chain and bracelet, and he had an unusual way of walking, insisting on having his hands in his trouser pockets all the time, thus limiting his speed. When friends pointed out how odd he looked he usually just laughed it off.

The day the attack happened, Brad was bunking off school. It was on a Monday. Not that this had any significance, since Brad treated himself to a day off whenever he felt like it. However, this particular day was to prove significant in the sense that Brad was going to commit a serious crime.

Brad was on his way to meet a friend who had called on his mobile to say that he too, had bunked off, when he noticed a woman getting off a bus down one of the side streets.

Forgetting the arrangement to meet his friend, Brad followed the woman, a short distance behind, taking care to avoid being noticed. There was a bakery at the corner of the road and the woman entered it. Brad walked casually past the shop, glancing in as he passed the doorway, briefly seeing the woman at the counter, obviously waiting to be served. Brad skipped around the corner and waited for the woman to come out of the shop and when she did, he resumed following her.

What was happening seemed unnervingly peculiar. He was following the woman without really knowing why. Brad thought she looked an ordinary woman in her mid thirties, not much older than his mother.

Suddenly, Brad felt a compulsion to approach her. Whilst he was wondering how he could do this, she turned from the road into one of the alleyways. Brad entered into the alleyway after her and then suddenly, a cloud of darkness descended upon him.

It only lasted seconds – but seemed like minutes. Brad grabbed hold of the woman's left arm and swung her around pinning her up against the wall. He did not speak as he lifted his right leg and lunged forward, bringing his genital area into contact with the same area on her. Despite the quickness and intensity of the shock, the woman, who was too frightened to speak or scream, mustered up enough courage and strength to push him away. She managed to do so with such force that Brad fell backwards and banged his head against the wall on the other side of the alleyway. The woman immediately fled the scene. Brad remained on the ground and did not attempt to follow her.

Brad returned home on the evening of the attack as if nothing had happened. He went into the kitchen and opened the fridge door to discover that there was little or no food to eat. Brad's mother's bedroom door was closed and so he could not determine by listening whether there was someone in there with her. So, he gently opened her door and saw that she was alone, asleep in bed. He then went to the living room, which was freezing cold, and slumped onto the sofa – and switching on the television, he sat watching it, with the hood of his top still over his head.

Brad lived in an unusual environment at home. His mother's ex-partner, who was the father to Brad and his brother, no longer lived with them and despite living in the same neighbourhood, none of them ever saw him. This did not really bother Brad, as he had never really formed a close bond with his father.

Brad's mother, on the other hand, had her hands full with a complex love life. Her promiscuous behaviour entailed her going through lover after lover. She was bisexual, with a tendency to switch from men to women almost on a rote basis. She found most of her conquests via the Internet. Some of these lovers stayed with her for a couple of days and others for a few weeks. Some behaved in a pleasant manner to Brad and his brother, whilst others chose to ignore them.

Brad had a riddle he often asked new friends: 'What's the difference between a whore and a slut?' he would question with a smirk on his face. 'A whore fucks everyone, whereas a slut would fuck everyone... except you!' – he would answer.

Brad often vocalised his thoughts that he considered his mother to be a slut.

Brad and his brother often spied on his mother's bedroom. They were accustomed to hearing lovemaking noises and they often made groaning noises as a means of annoying her, or as a response if she asked them to do something they didn't want to do.

Brad had started watching one of the teatime soaps. There was a scene in the programme where a mother was hugging her son. Brad did not know what had happened to the boy in the programme, who was crying, as he had missed the beginning. However, the scene being played before him grabbed his full attention. Tears swelled up in his eyes when he heard the comforting words of reassurance the mother was giving her son.

The scene hit a raw nerve for Brad as he reflected on how unloved he felt. He felt he wanted to be the boy in the programme and desired someone to care for him as much as the boy in the soap was being cared for. As the programme came to an end and music played to the final credits, tears streamed down Brad's face.

This was not the only extraordinary feeling that Brad would have that evening. After the programme had finished, he wiped his tears away but continued watching the television. However, whilst he continued staring at the screen, his attention drifted elsewhere. His thoughts turned to the attack he had carried out against the woman. For the first time he questioned himself about why he had done it. Brad tried to reason to himself that he was no rapist.

Considering the number of girls he fancied, he began to wonder whether he had actually fancied the woman or not. But thoughts of fancying an older woman did not occupy his thoughts for long, and he eventually surmised that what he had done had been a mistake – a stupid mistake.

This was the only explanation he could rationalise his actions with and recollections of the morning's events made Brad feel ashamed. Wondering what the woman must have thought of him turned to feelings of fear when he reasoned that she had probably gone straight to the police and reported what had happened. Panic grew within him as he realised that the woman would have given the police a description of him. Brad got up and went to the window. He asked himself what he could do – but few answers came. The thoughts of meeting the woman again, and her realising that it was he who had attacked her, made him feel very tense.

If this happened, Brad considered the possibility of approaching the woman and apologising. But he shook his head when he considered how foolish this would be. Besides she would either scream or run away – or reject his apology outright. Anyway, the dilemma of what to do would have to wait because at this moment his brother arrived home from school.

'Can't you be quiet?' Brad barked at his brother, who, coming in, had banged the door.

'Where is she?' asked his brother, referring to their mother.

'In bed, asleep.'

'So there's nothing to eat?' questioned his brother.

'Oh, what do you think?'

'Have you been crying?' the brother unexpectedly asked.

'I have not…now go and wake her and get some money for food. It's your turn to do the shopping,' Brad ordered to his brother.

Later that evening, Brad cooked spaghetti Bolognese for the three of them. He felt disgusted by his mother as she sat at the kitchen table in her nightdress, yawning profusely, whilst chain smoking. Attempts to stay calm and not make some type of derogatory remark, which would inevitably spark off a quarrel, proved difficult for him.

After the meal, as Brad was doing the washing up, he continued to ponder about how to rectify the mess in his life. He decided he would change his appearance, get a weekend job, stop bunking off school and pay more attention to his studies.

Then suddenly he was drawn to voices in the hallway. He looked out through the kitchen door and saw his mother taking a man he had never seen before into her bedroom. His heart sank at the sight.

Brad's despondency at seeing his mother taking a stranger into their home for more sex prompted him to go into the living room and sit down in silence. An overwhelming sense of emptiness came upon him, and enveloped him. He wondered why he should bother about changing anything in his life.

Chenai

Chenai could not get the previous night out of her mind. Thoughts raced through her mind about the way it had happened. She truly felt awful about herself and even the disinfectant in the bath could not make her feel clean. She had changed her bed linen but still could not bear to even sit on the bed. Restless and agitated she wanted the feelings to go away and to find some peace. Just a little peace, she reasoned, would make her feel better. Going for a walk was out of the question as she was still sore and besides, she had nowhere to go and the thoughts of wandering around the streets aimlessly weren't appealing. But she still craved peace. Anything at all to take away the horrible thoughts she was feeling about herself. She hadn't felt this despondent in ages and she desperately wanted to feel relief. It was at this point that she got out a small penknife that she had hidden in her wardrobe.

Chenai felt no pain as she stroked the blade across her wrists. In fact it had the opposite effect and the sensation of it made her instantly feel calmer. The room appeared brighter and she took this as the first indication that the dark cloud that had hung over her was about to lift. She continued cutting herself and only stopped when she saw that she was losing a lot of blood and feared that she might die if she lost any more. She reached for her pillow and took the cover off. She wrapped it around both wrists to stem the flow of blood. She did not feel any sense of panic as she had been in this type of situation several times before.

Drops of blood dripped from Chenai's wrists onto her legs and carpet. In fact, there appeared to be traces of blood everywhere in her bedroom. She walked around the room to gather her thoughts. She did not know how she would tell her parents. But she was beginning to feel calmer.

Chenai self-harmed almost on a continual basis but recently there had been a period when she had stopped. During her most distressed moments she scratched and scraped at her arms, wrists and thighs. Despite stringent measures taken by her parents to avoid access to harmful and sharp items, Chenai still found articles with which to cut herself. However, on this occasion, she had cut herself more than she had intended and knew that her wounds would need bandaging or perhaps medical attention. She realised that this would mean having to tell her parents.

Chenai's parents appeared very supportive but her mother had a tendency to over-react when she self-harmed. Tears, crying and bewilderment were the usual reaction from her mother. Chenai felt little sympathy for her mother's distress especially since telling her the reasons why she harmed herself. Her mother accused her of lying and threatened to disown her if she mentioned her 'nonsense' to anyone else. She also told Chenai that she brought shame to the family every time she had to be hospitalised as a result of her self-inflicted injuries.

Chenai knew that she would have to endure her mother's dramatics from the moment she left the safety of her room – and whisperingly mimicked to herself what she envisaged would be her mother's reaction:

'Oh Chenai...not again...why, why, why...do you keep doing this to yourself?'

Her father on the other hand, was always very sympathetic to Chenai and was prepared to console and support his daughter. He often attempted to give her a hug after she injured herself but Chenai would push him away. She was delighted that he was at work that evening and therefore would not have to face him.

Chenai wanted to be liked at school and made efforts to make friends. She was a bright girl, had a nice personality and knew everything there was to know about the latest trends in fashion and music. But it was the same with every friend she made. Chenai would show her wounds to her new friend, and this would instantly frighten and scare him or her away. None of her friends understood why she self-harmed as she could never muster the courage to actually tell them the reasons behind her scars. Therefore they distanced themselves from her and often dismissed her as odd by labelling her 'the freaky one'.

Chenai had guessed correctly. Her mother became hysterical when she saw the damage she had done to her wrists. Chenai watched her reaction and wondered why she kept up the denial. She had told her mother that she had to injure herself after 'it' had happened. During their confrontations on the subject this was the only way that Chenai could refer to the awfulness of the abuse she had been enduring for several years.

The cuts were really deep this time. Despite providing immediate first aid, Chenai's mother knew that the injuries needed stitches. Since Chenai's father was at work she telephoned a taxi to take them to the hospital. Some of the nurses in the casualty department remembered Chenai from previous occasions. However, her medical notes indicated that she had not been treated at the department in the last six months. This indicated a change in her state of mind.

'What has happened to you my dear?' the nurse treating her gently enquired.

Before Chenai got a chance to reply – her mother interjected and replied to the nurse:

'Oh, she has been a very silly girl.'

Then Chenai's mother turned around and addressed her:

'It's not serious darling… we'll have you out of here in no time at all after your stitches,' she excitedly told Chenai.

'Is there anyone you would like to speak to about your problems?' the nurse asked whilst bandaging Chenai's wrists.

'No, stop asking me questions,' Chenai responded in an agitated tone of voice when she realised the nurse was suspicious of her injuries.

'She's already seeing a school counsellor – terrible stress with her course work,' her mother replied on her behalf.

This was a complete lie as Chenai had never seen any counsellor, nor had she divulged the truth behind her injuries to anyone other than her mother.

Her mother had become calm as they waited in the waiting room for a taxi home. In fact, she had become really quiet and withdrawn.

It was almost as if she had gone into a trance. She was staring at the wall across from her.

'What's wrong, mum?' asked Chenai.

'Did he do "it" to you again?' her mother replied before bursting into tears.

Chenai's father had begun sexually abusing her four years previously. To begin with it happened weekly and then progressed steadily to an almost daily occurrence. Then it would stop for a while – sometimes for a few months before it started all over again. She had begged her mother time and time again to believe her but had failed to get through. Based on her mother's reaction this time she thought that maybe now she would finally be believed.

Chenai woke late the following morning. The nurse had given her painkillers which made her sleep continuously throughout the night. She wondered why her mother had not woken her. She panicked a little about missing lessons especially with her exams looming. This prompted her to get up quickly as she was determined not to miss school. Then she heard her parents talking and laughing in the kitchen. Chenai found herself trembling with disbelief. When she heard more laughter, she tried to reassure herself that this was not happening.

'What do you want for breakfast, darling?' her mother called out when she heard the bedroom door opening.

'I don't want anything,' Chenai quietly replied.

It was at this point that her heart began to sink. She realised that her mother had again failed to believe her and wondered if things would ever change. A quick exit from the house followed.

On her way to school, Chenai stared out of the bus window at various people walking to and fro on the pavement. Deep in her thoughts, she tried to imagine what their lives must be like. A woman walked past holding the hand of her child. Chenai felt an instant pang of jealousy towards the young girl, who was aged no more than five or six. The events that had caused her so much hurt and pain flashed through her mind.

Chenai's thoughts then turned towards her own mother as she asked herself if she would ever really believe her about her father. She consoled herself by thinking that this would eventually happen – and that when it happened her father would then leave home and both her mother and she could have a really good life together afterwards. The feeling of this happening did not seem quite real though when her thoughts turned to her father. Perhaps there was another way. Chenai imagined her father stopping the sex, apologising and her accepting his apology. Then they could carry on as a normal family and everything would be fine. She debated in her mind whether all of this could be possible. Chenai tried to visualise that one morning when her father would be shaving, he would take a good look in the mirror and realise what he was doing was wrong and would stop.

Chenai's thoughts were suddenly interrupted when the bus arrived at the school and she had to get off. There, ahead of her at the school gates were some girls from her class. Chenai knew some would condemn her when they saw the new bandages. They would even question her in a curious manner. The reality of each prospective scenario filled Chenai with dread. And it was the word 'dread' that summed up Chenai's life. What fate had in store for her remained uncertain. But for the moment she was doing her best to get through each day. She enjoyed any moment that proved to be a welcome distraction from the brutality that was lurking in the shadows of the place she knew as home.

Dan

Dan hated the new neighbourhood his mother and father had just moved into but was eager to discover who he could victimise in this new area. His long piercing blank stare could appear endless and Dan was well aware that it scared people. He liked having the ability to frighten others – and the power of seeing terror on the faces of his chosen victims proved to be the source of an adrenaline rush for him. It was the kind of recognition he had striven to attain.

Dan spotted his next victim in the local park and decided to rob him. However, he hadn't bargained that the boy, whom he perceived as younger and weaker than himself, would put up such a struggle – so he decided to stab him in the shoulder with the broken top of a bottle that he had in his pocket. Dan stood spreadeagled over the boy, holding the piece of broken glass close to his face, smirking as he did so.

There was no reason why Dan needed to stab the boy. Being stronger than his victim, he knew he would have eventually overpowered him without having to resort to this level of violence. But Dan wanted greater satisfaction from his robberies – and this meant more than merely robbing someone of their belongings – rather it meant terrorising his victims.

A normal family home life was not something Dan had ever experienced. His family life had entailed him moving around a lot and his parents had split up several times after violent and drunken outbursts. Usually however, they would live apart for a while, and then get back together again. Dan had observed every type of argument imaginable between his parents and had been a witness to punches, kicks and hair pulling. Dan usually lived with his father during his parents' splits and rarely went to school at such times. However, despite an erratic education he was a reasonably good reader and liked football and car magazines.

The new family flat was on the ninth floor of a council estate block. The previous tenants had left the flat in an appalling state. The move had taken place with such haste that the authorities hadn't had enough time to decorate or mend the broken fixtures. This didn't concern Dan's parents – especially his mother – as she was not particularly interested in being house-proud. Admittedly, she did say to Dan's father that the place needed a good lick of paint, but that was as far as it went.

Her greatest concern was the distance away from the off-licence. Being so high up meant that they were a long way from the shops – especially since the lifts were frequently vandalised and as a result, were usually out of use. Dan's family didn't even have a washing machine and with the local laundry being half a mile away, it meant that trips were infrequent.

Dan found it difficult to make friends. Every time they moved, he ended up not liking other teenagers – or they did not like him. He remarked to his mother that he thought young people in their new area were weird.

'Maybe they think the same of you,' she replied.

'Why?' asked Dan, shrugging his shoulders in disbelief at his mother's suggestion.

'Imagine if they knew how often you pissed your bed…what would they say to that?' she retorted.

Dan's mother often provoked Dan by saying things like this. There were times when he would have tears of anger and frustration in his eyes at what she said to him. He was never able to counter her taunts. Dan's father often told her to 'shut up' and stop criticising him – but these requests fell on deaf ears and usually resulted in a tirade of abuse being exchanged between his parents. Dan's bedwetting and the lack of proper laundry facilities wherever he lived meant that there was a constant musty smell of urine in his bedroom.

Dan felt upset by what his mother had just said and decided to go out. He did not have anywhere in particular to go but just wanted to get away from his mother's hostility. He cursed aloud at the broken lift and had no other option but to walk down the stairs. However, when he got to the ground floor he noticed two men, a woman and two boys standing at the entrance to the flats.

'Are you Dan?' one of the men in the group asked.

'What has that got to do with you?' Dan questioned.

'Quite a lot as a matter of fact,' the man calmly replied.

The speed and violence of the next few minutes were a blur in Dan's memory. The two men each got him in a wristlock and twisted his arms until he screamed with pain and begged them to let him go. One of the boys then punched him hard in the stomach, whilst the other boy gave him a powerful karate-style kick in the back. The woman squared up as close to Dan's face as she could get. He was still held in wristlocks at this time. She told him that what they were doing to him was part of his final warning. The second part would be delivered to his parents. They wanted him off of the estate within the next week or they would seriously maim him in a punishment beating.

The group responsible for the attack on Dan was the family of the boy he had stabbed in the park a few days beforehand. They had come to deliver the revenge they felt was his due. Over the years people on the estate had lost faith in the police and judiciary system and, instead, had determined a self-imposed right to take matters into their own hands.

Needless to say, when he returned to the flat, Dan did not receive much sympathy from his mother for his injuries. However, the events of the next few hours and days overshadowed his aching muscles as Dan's parents realised that the threat needed to be taken seriously after they discovered a written warning in their letter box.

Everything turned into a state of panic. The message of the vigilantes was clear, unless the family vacated the estate, Dan would be seriously injured – and the flat firebombed.

However, Dan's family had nowhere to go to. The council was not impressed with the story. Dan stood in their offices and listened to the housing officer tell his father that they had run out of places to re-house them and that they would have to stay in the present flat for the time being. Besides, they were advised that if Dan started to stay out of trouble, the vigilantes might not trouble them anymore in return. However, this didn't convince Dan, because he believed the warning to be real. And real it was. But this was not to be realised for several days. In the intervening time Dan continued to have violent and abusive arguments with his parents, particularly his mother.

'You know this is your fault entirely. This isn't the way we raised you,' she repeatedly told him in a self-righteous tone of voice. 'Now we have to move again because of what you did,' she added.

One taunt followed another and Dan threw several objects at her to alleviate his anger and frustration. There was simply no escape from her. He had to stay in either the kitchen or the living room because his mattress was soaking wet. The intense atmosphere continued at home for a few more days until Dan got so fed up indoors he decided to go out, though he knew he had to be careful. Dan knew that there was a possibility of a secret watch being in place for him, but he decided to brave it anyway.

There was nobody at the bottom of the stairwell or in the courtyard at the front of the flats but, just as he was about to turn the corner by the front entrance, he suddenly felt a tap on his shoulder.

'So you haven't decided to heed the warning, I see,' he heard a voice say as he turned around.

Right before him were the two men who had helped deliver the warning and beating to him a few days previously. However, this time they did not threaten him physically. Instead, one of the men opened a bag he was carrying and showed Dan a petrol bomb that was inside. Dan was told that this was going to be used on his parents' flat after the week's warning had elapsed – if they still weren't gone by that time. The two men then walked on by. Dan stood still and wondered what he should do. He felt frightened. The calmness and certainty in the men's voices made him realise that he and his parents would have to flee for their safety. There was no other alternative if they wanted to stay alive. But he wondered how he was going to tell them this, especially his mother.

However, he didn't have to tell them. After he got home from the short walk he had taken, his father told him that they were going to live with his grandmother for a few weeks. This would mean moving to another new area until the local council could re-house them in some other part of the county.

'But sure he'll mess up the bed in his nan's house in no time at all,' was all his mother contributed to the discussion on their imminent move.

And so they moved yet again to another area. The same pattern continued for Dan with him never being able to make friends in any place he went, and never gaining any stability at any particular school. Dan's mother blamed him for all of this, whilst Dan himself blamed everyone except himself. However, Dan concluded there were perks to the continuous moving to different addresses. In his opinion this earned him the right to test out his own special brand of violence towards strangers – whom he knew he would never be able to befriend. Sadly Dan had grown accustomed to this kind of life and as such had reached a point where he could no longer see any wrong in his actions.

Eugene

Eugene was very small for his age but this did not trouble him unduly as he was well able to defend himself from any potential bullying at school. However, he had seen that his small growth concerned his mother as she continuously highlighted the issue in front of others. On one occasion, during a family gathering, he felt immensely annoyed when she got out a tape measure and started comparing everybody's height. It came as no surprise to Eugene that he was the smallest. He was embarrassed that even his cousin, who was a couple of years younger, was taller.

There was something about Eugene that made him feel enormously envious of others who received new things. Whenever one of his brothers or sisters received a present for Christmas or a birthday, he would tamper with the article. It did not matter whether it was a new computer game or a mobile telephone; it would be rendered broken after Eugene had laid his hands on it. Eventually his siblings became frustrated and stopped allowing him near their possessions. But Eugene escaped from having his maliciousness exposed and just smirked any time one of them joked about him being giddy or careless with things.

Eugene's attention then switched to new cars. He decided to himself that they would not be so new if they had a scratch or two on them. So he equipped himself with a nail that he had got from his father's workshop and carried this around in his pocket. Whenever he saw a new car, he would scrape the nail alongside the driver's side of the car. Eugene fully realised the horror the owners would express on seeing the damage.

Eugene had a turbulent relationship with his parents – particularly his father. He steadfastly refused to obey them and put up constant resistance to doing his homework, tidying his room or helping with any other chores. He was a normal teenager in that respect but he answered his parents in a way that was unacceptable. When Eugene refused to do something he would blatantly tell his father to 'fuck off'.

Beatings from his father did not deter him and he would usually retaliate by more swearing or by kicking his father.

When aggressive situations arose at home his mother would attempt to pacify him by promising to buy him a present if he calmed down. If this did not work she would take his side against that of his father. It was never a question of her truly agreeing with Eugene, but she preferred this to having violence in her home. Besides, it was a method that sometimes worked to restore peace. But then Eugene became cunning and spiteful by initially refusing a present and then prolonging the dispute until concessions were made that went against the wishes of his father. Then afterwards he would wait for a while before going to his mother and saying:

'You said you were going to buy me a present,' before adding 'You can't change your promise now.'

But a time came when no offers of a present could pacify Eugene. He persisted in being objectionable at home and incited arguments between his parents and siblings at any opportunity. One evening, following a violent confrontation with his parents over his stealing money from his older sister, he stormed out of the house in a fury. This provided him with an opportunity to whinge to his friends, and it was also an excuse to get 'stoned', something he had already planned to do with three of his friends later that evening.

Eugene had discovered that the local cemetery was a good gathering point to meet up with his friends. The cemetery provided a safe haven for a quiet smoke, especially if one of them had acquired some cannabis. Eugene would perch himself up on a headstone and puff away contentedly on a 'joint'. The group found that if they went there after seven o'clock in the evening there would rarely be any visitors. He really felt like the captain of a ship as he sat on a headstone with his feet dangling.

On this particular evening he was full of bravado as he sat in his usual place and lit up a joint, telling his friends about the argument he had started before he bolted from his house.

'It's all fucking shit,' he repeatedly said.

Eugene was a bit fed up though that none of them had anything to drink.

'Not even a fucking can of lager amongst the lot of us,' he said to his friends.

There was a suggestion in his voice that it was everyone else's fault except his.

'Well, let's do something to liven the fucking evening up a bit,' he then suggested.

They discussed the option of going elsewhere to socialise but Eugene persuaded his friends from this choice. He decided that their entertainment was going to be found right there in the cemetery.

Eugene took the nail out of his pocket and scratched the backs of several tombstones. He enjoyed doing this as the nail just glided across the marble and left a distinct mark on each one. As he scratched, he noticed that there was a freshly dug grave close by ready for a burial next day. It had been covered with green plastic sheeting and the soil from the grave had been carefully arranged at the side of the open grave. He was undecided as to how this preparation could be sabotaged. One of his friends suggested filling in the grave but Eugene thought that this would be inadequate. Nevertheless, he gave the go ahead.

'Let's fill the fucking thing in with these things,' he said to his friends.

Eugene then uprooted a wreath with his foot from another grave he was standing on. Being very much the ringleader, he issued orders to his little army who ran, fetched and flung armfuls of wreaths into the new grave. He just stood and watched.

'That's fucking enough,' he announced after the grave was three-quarters full.

Eugene then began kicking in some soil on top of the wreaths and beckoned for the others to do the same. Satisfied that they had truly messed up the new grave, Eugene was now sure that whoever would be the first to discover the vandalism next day would be fuming with anger and disgust. Even more so if they found some excrement on top of the grave.

'If any of you want a fucking shit…now's the time and place,' he said before returning to his seat and lighting up another joint as he waited for the others to join him.

Eventually Eugene's head was spinning with the effects of the cannabis. It was now dusk so he suggested it was time they all went home. But then it occurred to him that a final bit of vandalism would round the evening off nicely. He noticed that there were some new cypress trees planted at the far end of the cemetery. He beckoned for the others to follow him and together they pulled up all the new plantings and scattered them over the surrounding area. As they climbed over the fence on their way out Eugene proudly announced to everyone that he thought they had at least caused a few thousand euro worth of damage during their escapade.

When Eugene woke up the next morning he heard neighbours in the kitchen talking about the vandalism in the cemetery. He couldn't fully hear what was being said but pieced together from bits of the conversation that the *gardai** were out in force looking for the culprits. This didn't frighten or daunt Eugene in the least. He pulled the duvet up around his head and, before going back to sleep, decided that all he had to do was deny any involvement if questioned over the matter.

Despite door-to-door enquiries from the *gardai*, and it being the focus of scandal in the whole community, the *gardai* hadn't so far approached Eugene. However, one of Eugene's older brothers had become suspicious. He had heard rumours that Eugene and his friends sometimes went to the cemetery to smoke cannabis – and believed the rumours because he knew what a little rascal his brother could be. Eugene did his usual trick when his brother confronted him over the matter and started shouting and swearing, prompting his mother to intervene in the argument. His mother was horrified at the suggestion that he was responsible in any way for the desecration of the cemetery

---

* *Gardai* - Gaelic word used in Ireland pertaining to the Police.

and promptly took Eugene's side in the dispute, which immediately settled him. But he knew from the look in her eyes that she was not fully convinced that he was telling the truth. It didn't matter, though, because he knew that she would back him up regardless.

The local paper ran front-page coverage on the vandalism. Eugene gave his usual smirk when he saw the headlines. He didn't give a damn about the distress he had caused. Eugene liked the new feeling of being famous, albeit unacknowledged. He suddenly realised that the vandalism in the cemetery hadn't been pre-planned but had made front-page headlines and began imagining what would happen if he and his friends planned to do something really big in advance.

'Now that idea needs more exploring,' he said out loud to himself.

He decided to go immediately and have a serious chat with his friends.

Fay

Fay's mother laid the cutlery very carefully on the table. She had just put potatoes in the oven to roast and did not want them to overcook. It didn't really matter the way the potatoes were cooked or anything else for that matter because her husband would always find fault with them. This was just one of his tactics in maintaining total control over his wife and children. He belittled his wife's efforts in every way he could, especially in front of Fay and her siblings. Whatever type of meal she cooked for dinner he would ask why it was not something else. Likewise with the dessert, he always wanted something different from what was prepared.

Fay observed her father belittling her mother's appearance in the same manner. If she wore make-up he would say she looked like a 'tart'. Fay hated the contradictions in her father's statements and loathed the way her mother was berated for not making an effort in her appearance, or the way that she was condemned when she tried. The house was either too clean or not clean enough. Fay saw her mother lose contact with all of her old friends because her father hated the people in her mother's social circle and criticised them continuously.

Fay was the eldest child and felt responsible for what was happening within the family home even though she was helpless to protect her mother, brothers and sisters and, most of all, herself. It was one thing contending with her father's foul-mouthed tirade but there were also the beatings to endure. Everyone in the house received their turn if they did not do exactly as he said. Fay witnessed how her mother put up no resistance to her father's outbursts and often heard her apologise for her efforts.

Fay knew though that her mother tried her hardest to keep the home and family running smoothly. Fay's heart grew colder and colder towards her father every time she saw him beat her mother to the point where she would be all cuts and bruises. Eventually she hated her father so much that she wished he would fall off some scaffolding at the building site where he worked and be killed. She often referred to her home circumstances as '*Living with Hitler*'.

Fay began to stay out late at night as her father increasingly turned his venom towards her. Andrew, an older friend of Fay, told her one day that she looked very miserable and needed cheering up and that he had exactly what was needed to make this happen. She was given a valium tablet. She didn't know what to expect but swallowed it anyway out of curiosity.

That particular night Fay was terrified of returning home. Knowing her father would beat her for being out without his permission, she decided to accept another valium tablet from her friend. After taking it, her mood became elated and before long she was bursting with energy. Fay was led into believing that it would be great fun if she stole a car and went for a drive.

Andrew dared her into stealing a car by putting on a bet. She jokingly retorted that this was exactly what she would do – provided he'd pay the bet after she had won. They didn't have to walk far before an opportunity presented itself. A new sports car nearby had its keys left in the ignition. Fay couldn't believe her luck and commented on how idiotic it was for the owner to be so careless.

Although she had only driven twice before, she knew the basics. After starting the car she suddenly felt a surge of pleasure as she pressed her foot on the accelerator. The car glided under her and gradually increased its speed intensifying the sensation of freedom. Her hair was billowing in the wind. The excitement and the feeling of freedom were exhilarating. She was truly enjoying every moment of it. But her new found feeling of glee was cut short when she noticed a police car following her. Panic caused her to take a sharp turn on a roundabout and then, in a moment of insanity, she drove straight in the direction of the oncoming patrol car, which managed to swerve in time to avoid a head-on collision. However, both cars hit each other's wings and the windscreen in the patrol car was smashed to smithereens with the force of the impact. Thankfully, no one was seriously injured but the police officers sustained cuts from the broken glass.

However, Fay's joyriding was still not over. She had remained oblivious to what had happened and kept revving the accelerator although the car was now stationary. The feeling of euphoria was still running through her system. Then all of a sudden she fell into fits of hysterical laughter. She laughed and laughed uncontrollably until she eventually lost consciousness. She remembered nothing of the incident when she woke up the next day in hospital.

When she opened her eyes her parents were sitting by her bedside. The consequences of her alcohol and valium intake were about to be realised. It was the stern look on her father's face that caught her attention. She hadn't a clue where she was or what had happened to her. She felt no pain but her head was spinning and the room seemed so white and bright. Her father waited for the doctor to leave before threatening Fay with a beating when he got her home.

'You fucking little bastard, you will be taught a lesson once and for all,' he hissed as he jabbed a finger into his daughter's stomach.

'I'm sorry, Dad,' Fay responded.

Fay remained motionless in bed and kept her eyes closed, partly because of the bright light but mainly to conceal the fear she was feeling inside. There was nobody who could ease her mental anguish and protect her – and there was nobody who she felt cared for her right at that moment.

Fay didn't know what the future held for her. As the days went by she became very despondent when Andrew, whom she felt should share in the responsibility of her predicament, hadn't visited her in hospital. There was the strong possibility of her being convicted of a serious offence and in this respect she tried her best to blank out the horrible thoughts that flashed across her mind. Accepting responsibility for stealing the car and driving recklessly was a major source of concern.

But there was something worse than this troubling Fay. She knew that a time would come when she would eventually have to return home. This thought made her feel nauseous. Yet this was the only place she knew as home and had nowhere else with which she could make a comparison. However, this made Fay wonder if prison would be any worse than home? Whether anywhere else would be better than returning to a home filled with violence and which was under the leadership of the tyrant, simply wasn't a choice open to Fay just yet – but she knew that her impending court appearance might determine otherwise.

Gerry

Gerry had two sides to his personality. He was very proud of his family background. His father and four brothers all had criminal records. Gerry liked the word 'criminal'. It conjured up a status, which he found appealing to him. It also opened up doors in certain quarters for him, particularly when getting half-price cigarettes. An occasional 'eighth' of cannabis was often thrown in free when he paid cash up front to his cigarette suppliers. Gerry rather liked this little perk.

The other side to Gerry was a likeable little boy. He loved animals, particularly dogs. He would have loved a black Labrador but, unfortunately, his father wouldn't allow it. Planes also fascinated him, and although he had never flown in one, he thought whoever invented them was a genius. Gerry also liked the idea of learning to be an engineer. Then he would be able to fix the engines of huge jumbo jets.

Gerry's family shielded a little secret. One of his uncles had sexually abused him when he was ten. One day his uncle had followed him into the bathroom and started masturbating in front of him. The uncle then persuaded Gerry to take out his penis and asked him to imitate what he himself was doing. Gerry did so and this resulted in him having his first ever ejaculation in front of his uncle. It was only after Gerry told one of his brothers about the 'weird' things that his uncle was doing that he discovered that his brother had also been asked, in the past, to do similar things.

Life was difficult in the family home. Gerry's parents had separated and he seldom saw his mother whose visits were infrequent now that she had started a new relationship. There was no order in the house since Gerry's older brother Tony had been sent to prison. Gerry liked Tony the best of all his brothers because he was good at cooking as well as settling disputes in the home.

Gerry's tantrum outbursts were totally unpredictable. Sometimes he would object strongly to the smallest thing. This would happen if he was asked to do something trivial or if one of his brothers was watching something on the television and he wanted to watch a programme on another channel. Whenever this happened he would end up shouting, screaming abuse and breaking objects in the house.

Gerry was counting the days for Tony to come out of prison but there was still eight months to go before his release. In the meantime he passed his time socialising with friends who lived on the same estate. The railway station was the local place where young people met up. They favoured this because there were always a lot of people about and, if it was raining, they were able to shelter under the station's large canopy.

They played several pranks on people coming in and out of the station. Sometimes they would drink a can or two of lager, intensifying the bravado amongst them.

One day Gerry saw a respectable middle-aged woman coming out of the station. She resembled his French teacher at school.

'Excuse moi, Madame…what is the French for this?' he called out to her as he partially exposed his penis.

'Oh grow up,' replied the woman.

One silly prank followed another until Gerry got bored and decided to do something else to liven things up a bit. It was a cold evening and he suggested to his friends that they make a little fire. He was surprised by the look on their faces and realised they hadn't a clue what he was talking about. Gerry told them about a derelict house that was a few hundred metres from the station. He convinced them that it would be a good idea to set fire to it and encouraged them to help him steal petrol from a nearby car. Gerry suggested they could put the petrol in the empty lager cans they had earlier discarded.

Gerry and his friends approached the house. The windows were all boarded up but the front door was partly open. The street lighting failed to penetrate the interior but there was just enough light to enable them to spill petrol over the floorboards and staircase. Gerry ordered everyone to light a match – and on the count of three, for them all to throw their matches onto the fuel. Flames soon spread as Gerry and his friends ran away from the scene. They decided to stay away for a quarter of an hour and then come back when the house was engulfed in flames – and when other people would have also gathered around. Gerry thought this would eliminate them from being associated with lighting the fire.

When Gerry and the others returned, the fire brigade had arrived and were trying to quench the flames that had engulfed the house. There was a small group of people gathered outside the burning building.

'I hope old Jack is not in there,' Gerry overheard a woman say to one of the fire officers.

'Do you think there may be someone in the building?' the fire officer asked.

'There is a local elderly homeless man that sometimes sleeps in there,' the woman replied.

Unbeknown to Gerry, a homeless man used the empty dwelling to sleep in sometimes. Nobody knew if he had been in the house when the fire started. Gerry froze with terror. He could feel his legs almost go from under him. Although all his friends had helped to set the fire, it was his idea in the first place and now an innocent man may have lost his life because of his stupidity.

Gerry decided to quickly get away from the place. He was sick with worry about the possibility he could be responsible for someone's death. He couldn't bear to wait around and listen to more of the conversation between the woman and fire officers. Returning home in a restless state he spent the remainder of the evening agonising about what would happen if the homeless man had perished in the fire.

The next day Gerry was delighted to find out that his fears had been in vain when the news got back to him that the homeless man had been seen alive and well in town. Gerry breathed a silent sigh of relief. He had felt consumed by guilt at the imagination that it was his match that had first ignited the fire despite his friends throwing their matches at the same time as he had done.

Gerry was beginning to gradually accept that what he had done could have had disastrous consequences and that luck must have been on his side. But he also began to realise that luck cannot be taken for granted. Therefore, he resolutely made up his mind never to get involved in a prank like this again. Perhaps he was indirectly taking on board the advice given to him by the lady outside the railway station after his indecent exposure. The time had indeed come for him to grow up and Gerry himself was beginning to realise this. He made a pact with himself that he would be completely changed by the time Tony came out of prison.

Hugh

Hugh was a very good talker. In fact people often complained that he talked too much. He had taken some LSD when he was younger and had never really recovered from the effects. Hugh also suffered mood changes and was constantly arguing with his friends and carers. He had lived in a children's home for nearly a year and hated every minute of it. One of the reasons for his unsettled behaviour was his constant bickering with others. Hugh could never understand anyone who was different from himself, and could never appreciate viewpoints that didn't conform to his.

Hugh was a very ordinary looking youth in appearance but had a very over-rated opinion of himself. He felt that girls were very attracted to him and wore Christian Dior aftershave that his mother had bought him, believing that this would get him noticed. But when he did get noticed it was usually for the wrong reasons. His peers in the community criticised him behind his back, because Hugh had gained a reputation for exaggerating and lying and was therefore seldom believed when he boasted. He even tried to convince his friends that his family were rich and that one of his uncles was a judge but they just laughed at his sentiments.

It was a wet day when things came to a head. Hugh and the other children had stayed indoors because of the bad weather. He hated this, as he and his friends would normally be in town at this time of evening, catching up on excitement or creating their own brand of it. This was usually found in the shopping malls or in the games emporium on the slot machines. Hugh had been given some cannabis the previous day and decided to arrange an impromptu party in his bedroom. Four other boys joined him. They were a little younger than he was so his make-believe stories made an impression on them. Hugh lit the 'joint' and passed it in turn to the other boys in the group. Some of them were eager to smoke it as it was their first time and were keen to experience the sensation of the drug.

All was going well until a member of staff interrupted the party and found Hugh and his friends smoking cannabis. When challenged it soon became clear to staff who was the ringleader. In fact, Hugh didn't deny his involvement.

'So what do you think you can do about it, you prick?' was his reply to the staff member.

Hugh was asked to stay in his bedroom. He lay on the bed and sulked. The staff told him that he had to be punished for what he had done – and that this would entail him having to do extra kitchen duties for a week. He put up an almighty argument against this because he felt that he was being blamed for everything when it wasn't entirely his fault. He disputed that he had forced the others to smoke and maintained that they had wanted to try it themselves. Hugh challenged this point over and over again, but the staff reminded him that he had lived there long enough to know the rules and that the only option available to him was to abide by them.

Later that evening, Hugh played his usual trick of telephoning his mother and telling her a fabricated story. He knew that she would be supportive, as she always appeared to believe his stories about occurrences in the home. Hugh's mother would challenge the staff after he had told her his version of the day's events. Thus, he reported to her that the staff were picking on him, yet again, for nothing. He told his mother that it was not he who had started the cannabis party and added that he was being bullied at the home and that staff did not care about him, that nobody liked him and that he always got blamed and punished for things that were not his fault. It was no surprise when his mother reiterated her belief in him and said she would do something about him being wrongly blamed.

The reason Hugh's mother took his side and was protective of him was because she felt guilty about not being a good mother. This was irrespective of whether she believed his tales or not. Hugh knew her motive because he had once overheard a conversation between his mother and an aunt. He knew his mother felt guilty about what had happened to him when he was younger. She had severely neglected him as she battled drug addiction and was still haunted by the memories of seeing him in court the day she was sentenced to prison. The vision of seeing Hugh crying and clinging to her sister as she was led away to the cells, remained in her mind to the present day, stirring up emotions of remorse and failure. But little did Hugh's mother know that it was at this precise point in the courtroom that he had subconsciously started to plot his revenge to one day punish her for the pain and suffering she had caused him.

She now thought that if she did not side with him in disputes that he would reject her again. Initially this had happened after she had come out of prison. When she first went to see him at the children's home, he did not want anything to do with her and demonstrated great animosity. Their relationship was now improving, partially because his mother was working and could buy Hugh the clothes and footwear that he wanted.

The manager of the children's home tried his best to talk the situation through with Hugh's mother over the telephone and tell her exactly what had happened. It was at this point that Hugh passed the office door and overheard the conversation. He instantly realised that his mother wasn't prepared to believe what the manager was telling her. Hugh was right to believe that she always took his side without much persuasion. He rejoiced in the belief that he had won again and grinned with satisfaction. Lies worked for him every time and he had no intention of changing his game plan when he had his mother as an excellent accomplice.

But events were about to take a turn for Hugh. After the conversation with Hugh's mother, the manager held a staff meeting where it was decided that a different type of action would take place. Hugh, being suspicious of the meeting, initiated an eavesdropping session by the door whereby he and some of the other boys took turns to pass by. Stories came back to Hugh that the staff agreed that they were frustrated by the level of blame and criticism that his mother directed towards them. They wondered if she was fully aware of all the details about his behaviour. The manager was going to write to her and invite her to a meeting. This was considered the best way to discuss recent and previous incidents in Hugh's presence – and therefore curtail his lying.

When Hugh found out about the proposed meeting he indeed feared his lying ways would be exposed. He wondered what further fabrications he could make up to exonerate himself. Worried and anxious, he kept asking staff what was going to be discussed at the meeting with the manager and his mother. He had cried wolf so many times to his mother and it had worked perfectly. Was this going to be his last time? Would his behaviour improve after the meeting, or would he have to change tactics and adopt a different style of behaviour to suit his ways?

The outcome of the meeting remained to be seen. In the meantime Hugh decided that there was little point worrying about things and decided to forget about them by going into town to meet up with some friends at the games emporium. He considered to himself that he might have better luck on the games machines than he was having in the children's home. Besides, he consoled himself with the hope that he would come up with a way of wriggling himself free from his predicament.

A little voice at the back of Hugh's head kept repeating that his mother owed him; that she was obliged to come to his defence – whose fault was it that he was stuck in this wretched stinking hellhole of a children's home? The voice told him over and over again that if she had been a proper mother that he would be living with her in a nice house, that he would be normal – and would be happy and have nice friends.

Indiana

Indiana liked people to call her by this nickname. Her real name was 'Miremba' but few people ever called her that now. She lived with her father in a tiny flat. The council had moved them after her parents had separated. Indiana knew that her father hated living in Britain – because she had grown up listening to his disapproval of British customs and morals. She thought that it served him right that he hated the country so much and put her feelings for him on a par with those he had for his adopted country. However, her father's health had deteriorated from the chronic arthritis that afflicted him. Again, Indiana thought he deserved to be sick and felt her feelings were justified. He was a very authoritarian man and his temperament was the cause of his wife's return to Uganda, taking Indiana's younger brother with her.

Indiana constantly rebelled against her father's rules at home. However, since his health had declined, this resulted in him not being able to challenge her behaviour any longer – so Indiana had become accustomed to doing whatever she wanted. She had a very domineering personality and enjoyed bullying peers who were smaller than her or whom she perceived as being weaker in character. She had the ability to quickly discover people's weaknesses and exploit them.

Once Indiana observed a girl at school being bullied by some other girls. She befriended the girl under the pretext that she would protect her from the perpetrators if the girl agreed to pay for this service. She asked for the money up front but failed to protect her as promised. Instead of protecting the girl she continued to demand daily amounts of money, telling her if she didn't comply that she would tell the bullies to increase their level of torture. In the end, the girl was both bullied and blackmailed with Indiana remaining completely oblivious to the girl's suffering.

One day Indiana had arranged to go into the city centre with some of her friends. She was late getting up and slammed the front door shut as she raced towards the bus stop. Indiana was dressed in her usual attire consisting of jeans, sweatshirt and trainers. She had very short hair and wore a baseball cap. She looked very much a tomboy and had no interest in hair or make-up. Indiana preferred being in male company, more than being with other females.

The friends waiting for her at the bus stop were two boys of her own age.

'You didn't call me last night, you cock sucker,' she yelled at one of the friends.

An elderly woman standing at the bus stop glanced in her direction.

'What are you looking at, you old git?' Indiana shouted at her.

Indiana suddenly noticed a boy of about ten coming out of a newsagent's shop directly across from the bus stop. Indiana was very tall and well built for her age and knew full well that her size intimidated younger children. Indiana instantly recognised the young boy as an easy target. She beckoned to her friends to join her across the road.

'What have you got there, you little white trash?' she yelled at the boy.

'Nothing,' he replied.

'Listen here, you little white trash, empty out your pockets or I'll break your neck,' were her next words as she took the ice cream from his hand and threw it on the ground.

The boy started crying. Indiana's reaction was to strike out and hit him across the head making him cry louder. She emptied out his pockets and found an iPod.

'Little white trash is a liar as well as a cry baby,' she yelled, as she considered how much she would get if she sold the iPod.

At this stage several people on the street had heard the commotion and were coming out of shop doorways to see what was happening.

'Leave the lad alone,' a local shopkeeper called out from his shop.

'Don't you mess with me! When people mess with me I'll show them exactly what I think of them,' Indiana replied.

There was a woman passing by on the opposite side of the street. She called out to Indiana to stop terrorising the young boy. The woman crossed the road to make sure that the boy was rescued.

Indiana didn't like her authority being challenged like this, especially as she didn't want to appear weak in front of her friends. As the woman approached them Indiana struck out and hit her hard across the face before running off with her friends down an alleyway. The young boy was still in tears after she fled because the iPod had been a Christmas present from his grandmother.

Indiana was in a foul mood when she got home. She despised the downloads that were on the iPod and flung it hard against the kitchen wall destroying it in the process. On the same day, her father's arthritis was particularly painful which rendered it difficult for him to walk. He would have liked a cup of tea but discovered they had run out of milk. Indiana completely ignored him when he asked her to go and do some shopping. Ignoring her father was her usual way of dealing with their communications. Besides, she had already eaten at a friend's house and thought to herself that if her father wanted some shopping that he should go and do it himself. After all, she considered that her father had split the family up and she was determined that he must suffer for this.

Instead of going to the shops for her father she decided to take a bath. As the water was filling up she put on a CD and turned the volume up high. Her father's protests about the loudness went un-noticed.

'Turn that stupid music down,' he shouted down the hallway.

'Shut up – you don't have to listen to it if you don't want to,' Indiana bellowed back to him.

With this, Indiana locked the bathroom door and continued with her bath. She felt it was his problem if he didn't like the volume or choice of music. She reasoned if he was so bothered by it, he could always go out and do the shopping that he was moaning about. This was life for Indiana. Misery and bitterness had entirely replaced any form of love and affection between her and her father – and in this mode she drifted from day to day.

Jake

Jake sat in the bus shelter and stared at his vomit. Its smell, mixed with the odour of alcohol, disgusted people as they passed, but he remained oblivious. His mind was completely transfixed on a nightmare he had had the previous night. In it, a man stood at the door of his house telling him that his *'mother was going to die, too'*. After being given this warning, the man attempted to shake hands but they kept missing each other. It was only after several attempts that they managed to link and Jake could still vividly feel the clammy hand that clasped his own.

Jake's mother had died two years previously so the message did not make sense. What he couldn't understand about the dream was the emphasis the man put on the word 'too'. In his drunken state he wondered if it was some kind of warning that either his father or sister, with whom he lived, were going to die soon. The thought of either of them dying made him tearful. Jake began to get so distressed he almost missed his bus, just managing to snap out of the trance and jumping up before the doors closed.

Jake was on his way to meet Celina, his girlfriend. They had a turbulent relationship, which was often prompted by his carefree attitudes towards relationships and sex. But they always managed to patch up their difficulties one way or another. In fact, since his mother died he had felt more a part of his girlfriend's family than his own. Jake got along terrifically with her parents, particularly Celina's mother who had become a replacement mother figure in his life. Football results dominated his conversations with Celina's father. Overall Jake spent a lot of time at Celina's house, enjoying the cosy atmosphere that he no longer felt in his own home.

He knew that Celina tolerated his infidelities to the point where she pretended that they hadn't happened. However, stories continually reached her that he was unfaithful. The previous weeks had seen them row continuously about flings behind her back. During some of these heated disputes Jake inflicted bruises to her arms and shoulders from the blows he struck. Nonetheless, they usually managed to kiss and make up and appeared to continue afterwards as if nothing had happened.

Jake was beginning to sober up a little after he got off the bus. He had arranged to meet Celina at the cinema. He wasn't very fazed by her complaints that he smelt of alcohol. The only thought on his mind was to have a fun evening. He decided to liven things up a little so he began to get louder and louder in the ticket queue. He started shouting about the length of the queue.

'Why the fuck is this thing held up…I'm bursting for a piss,' he aggressively announced.

Then, placing a hand around Celina's shoulder, he attempted to sing a song that he pretended to be composing as he sang.

He knew he wasn't a very good singer but persevered nevertheless to sing his own version of the Kaiser Chiefs' song '*My girlfriend loves me…and my girlfriend's parents love me.*'

Some people in the queue laughed at him but he was unaware of this. His attempts to fine tune his impromptu song continued but others in the queue were less impressed by his loud antics.

Jake stopped when a man two positions ahead of him turned around and said to him 'Put a sock in it, mate.'

It was at this moment that Jake's temper became aroused and he then did something that would change his life and the lives of others around him forever.

Jake had taken to carrying a knife around with him over the previous months but this was the first occasion that he felt the need to use it. Friends knew he carried a knife and Jake enjoyed the 'hard man' image it evoked within his social circle. It had become a bit of a fashion accessory to him and he liked the authority that he assumed when it was on his person.

'What the fuck did you say to me?' Jake yelled out at the man.

The man didn't reply to Jake. Not being content with this, Jake decided to move forward and square up to the man. The man took a step backwards when Jake entered his personal space. Attempts to explain to Jake that he was being a nuisance didn't go down too well. Jake really didn't understand what the man was talking about and started shouting at him. Jake considered he was only prancing around and trying to have a bit of fun with his girlfriend. He resented the man showing him up in front of his girlfriend and others in the queue – and decided that the man needed to be taught a lesson to stop him poking his nose into other people's business.

Jake reached to his inside pocket, took the knife out, and stabbed the man in the shoulder. All of this happened fast. Jake had never stabbed anyone ever before. He only carried the knife as a deterrent to frighten people and never actually meant to use it – and because of this he was quite unprepared for what happened afterwards.

At the precise moment that Jake stabbed the man some realisation clicked in him that what he had done was wrong. But it was too late. He had done it and could see the man's blood coming through his clothes. Celina started screaming. Someone else shouted to call an ambulance and the police. Others around started to grab at Jake but failed when he retaliated. Besides, he had a knife and this was a more effective deterrent than any blow or kick. There was no time to think. Events were spiralling out of control. Jake fled the scene as quickly as he could.

The real nightmare had begun, or so it seemed. Jake was accustomed to nightmares though and had been living one since his mother's death two years previously. He missed her and felt life had changed so much afterwards that nothing seemed to matter. He had failed at school and subsequently dropped out. There was no job that interested him. He had found some solace with his girlfriend and her family, but there was something about this situation too that didn't seem real. He didn't love Celina, and had to blank out the thoughts of hitting her. Jake had more or less conceded to himself that he was a failure. He often joked to himself that he was never much of a scholar but was pleased that he had learned how to spell the word 'LOSER' – because this would come in useful when he would have it tattooed across his forehead.

Jake

Stabbing the stranger in the cinema queue just intensified his despondent feelings. Jake sat on a shop doorstep a couple of streets away from the scene he had earlier fled. Knowing that it would only be a matter of time before the police picked him up, he sat there in a self-pitying manner. He questioned what the point to anything was and wondered if he would be better off dead. But he wasn't suicidal and didn't want to kill himself. Perhaps, he thought, there was someone out there who could help him. It might only be a matter of him allowing his side of the story to be heard.

It was a long story. It covered the seven hundred and seventy days since his mother's death. The story contained dreams that she was still alive, nightmares that she came back for a while but died again, more nightmares that she wanted to come back to life but couldn't do so. Then Jake had recurring flashbacks to the day she died – all of which were in vivid detail. The grief, loneliness and despair were deep but the deepest anguish of all was simply missing her.

Jake felt that people wouldn't be interested in his life story now that he had stabbed someone. He reasoned they would be more interested in getting him locked up for what he had done. After all, he reasoned, that's what you do to people who stab others. You lock them up and write 'LOSER' across their foreheads.

'Will anyone ever believe in me?' he wondered, as he watched for the patrol car to come and collect him.

Kenny

Kenny had never known who his father was and this had exerted a profound affect on him. He never smiled and gave the appearance of someone who had never experienced any happiness or joy in his life. His mother used to constantly get upset when he asked her about his father, whose identity was never established as his mother had a string of different lovers. Kenny secretly wondered what his father would be like and wanted to imagine him as a good man. He certainly did not want him to be like his present stepfather who drank heavily and often hit him when under the influence of drink and drugs.

Kenny's mother had never acted as a good role model in his life. His mother and his stepfather had a serious drug habit, which made them extremely violent at times. They often vented their anger on Kenny, especially his mother when he asked at inopportune times about his father's identity. He often did this when his mother was busy arranging parties at their flat. On these occasions Kenny was ignored more than usual and was often yelled at to 'shut up' by his mother.

Several drug parties took place in their flat – with abundant supplies of crack cocaine and heroin available. Crowds of people would come to these events, which continued sometimes over the course of a couple of days. The guests would invariably sleep anywhere, be it on a spare sofa or on a rug once they had their fill of drugs and alcohol. During these parties, Kenny was made to stay in his bedroom. If he attempted to come out his mother or stepfather would shout at him and tell him to go back inside, only ever briefly letting him out to go to the toilet before getting quickly ushered back in again. There were times when he begged to come out of the room and go outdoors but his pleas went unnoticed. It was not unusual for Kenny to go without food or anything to drink for two days at a time. Whilst he was not allowed to come out of the room, people who came to the parties often strayed into his room. It was not unusual for them to have sex with each other if they thought Kenny was asleep. He was rarely asleep and knew exactly what was happening.

Eventually a neighbour reported the situation to the police and Social Services became involved. Kenny ended up going to live with his aunt and her partner. He generally liked his aunt Louise. They always related well to each other and she was kind to him, often buying him clothes and games he liked. However, once Kenny had moved in with his aunt his character began to change, resulting in argumentative and rude behaviour.

Initially, he would play a charade on his aunt by getting up each morning and pretending to go to school – but later on, after she discovered the truth, he shouted at her, 'Fucking school… I hate it… I'm not going any more and no-one is going to make me.'

One part of Kenny took advantage of living with his aunt. It was as if this new-found freedom gave him reason to lose his temper or to disobey his aunt whenever she attempted to enforce discipline. But the other part was his naivety and his ability to be easily led. He liked the recognition that bravado earned him from his associates and was easily enticed and influenced by them.

One evening Kenny went into a shop with a knife on his person. He asked the Asian shopkeeper to open the till and to give him the contents. He also demanded some cigarettes be handed over. Two of his accomplices stood guard at the front door. The shopkeeper refused Kenny's requests and told him that she would set her German Shepherd dog on him if he did not leave immediately.

'I'm not afraid of your fucking dog, you p*** bitch!' Kenny replied, 'I'll stab you both now if you don't do as you're told. Give me the money out of the till! Fill a bag here with cigarettes,' he ordered.

He scraped the knife across the counter by the till and then held out the knife directly to the shopkeeper's eye level. She considered there was no alternative but to comply with his demands.

Kenny left the shop and fled from the scene with his two friends. Part of him felt exhilarated by what he had just done. He had enjoyed the thrill of getting the shopkeeper to do as he had commanded. He did not feel guilty about what he had done to the woman shopkeeper – and readily justified his actions to his friends.

'Well she got what was coming to her…mum has always said that people like her shouldn't be in this country anyway because that's why British people can't get jobs,' he muttered.

Events at home with aunt Louise were proving problematic. His behaviour had deteriorated more and by the time of the robbery, Kenny had reached the point where he completely disobeyed his aunt. He would often return home drunk or under the influence of cannabis. On these occasions he would act rudely and be disrespectful to his aunt and often spat at her when she challenged him over his behaviour. He moaned that he was bored and had nothing to do. Kenny told her that he wanted to go back and live with his parents. He accused her of being a control freak and that all she wanted to do was rule him like his parents had. He used to say these things to her because he knew that she would relent to his tantrums.

Kenny's aunt was emotionally at breaking point. It had put a strain on her relationship with her partner. She did not know what was best to do. She knew that he could not be allowed back to live with his parents – not for the time being anyway, until their problems were under control. On the other hand, she realised that things could not continue as they were. She had heard stories about the way he behaved in town with his friends and how their activities were often criminal.

Reluctantly, Kenny's aunt decided that her only option was to ring his social workers and inform them that she could no longer cope – and to ask for him to be accommodated elsewhere. It was not that she did not love or care deeply for Kenny. Perhaps what saddened her most was the realisation that Kenny did not show any care for anyone – and that he would not be bothered if he was asked to leave her home.

Kenny was told by his aunt of the possibility of being taken into foster care but he didn't believe she would go ahead with this. He decided to be very rude to two social workers who came around to do the assessment. Kenny made them very much aware that whether he was put into foster care or not, he would continue to go out and meet his friends, drink and smoke cannabis if he felt like doing so. He added that he didn't care about their disapproval because he was free to choose to do whatever he liked.

'I'm not the one with the problem here,' he flippantly stated.

'It's certainly not me that's doing this to you – sit down and talk,' his aunt replied.

'Yeah, it is your problem and I couldn't give a fuck about it,' came his reply. 'You were the one that said you were going to look after me,' he added.

Kenny's aunt began to cry. He was pleased he had stood his ground and that this had weakened her resolve. His aunt asked the social workers whether they could put the fostering on hold for a while, as she was willing to give Kenny another chance. It made him chuckle when he heard his aunt say that maybe they might be able to come to some type of compromise over his behaviour.

Kenny looked at his watch. It was time for him to go out. He sarcastically implied to the social workers that he had more important things to attend to but they could continue with their little conversation in his absence. After he left the house Kenny felt like he had left people behind who were discussing someone else. But it wasn't someone else they were discussing – it was him.

But Kenny was far too preoccupied with anticipation of the date that he was heading off to. So remote was the situation with his aunt at home that it wasn't even second place in his thoughts. It simply wasn't registering. He felt he was in charge of his own life and didn't feel that he needed her concern. He considered that he was capable of taking care of himself and that this was all he needed to survive. However, the reality was that Kenny was quickly turning into a young man whose life was veering more and more out of control every day – and the downward spiral showed no signs of stopping.

Libby

Despite being in her early teens, Libby came across as being very young and immature in years. The friends who she hung out with were older and more street wise. Often she would just sit in a listless manner. She was the type of girl who would stand out in a crowd because she was quieter than her friends. At times when she was in the company of others she would suck her thumb as she stared into empty space. Her vulnerability shone through and her social skills clearly indicated someone who had had a difficult upbringing. Libby's nails were badly bitten and she had a blank expression on her face that denoted some-one who had suffered a great deal emotionally. Her unassuming nature increased her level of vulnerability. Unbeknown to her she was being recognised in her group as easy prey and that predators were waiting to pounce on her at any moment.

Home life for Libby was unimaginably grim. Her mother died whilst she was still a young child. Her father drank quite heavily. He accumulated mounting debts from a gambling habit. She had seen his personality go from fun loving and caring to someone who had become very depressed. This eventually affected his level of care towards his family and resulted in Libby and her brothers becoming completely neglected. Libby was very much left to her own devices. This meant that she was never taught how to wash properly and was poorly nourished as a result of often relying on one meal a day.

One day, her father came home drunk. He looked at Libby and for the first time recognised that she was growing up into a beautiful young woman. Moving closer to her he started fondling her breasts. Libby froze with fear and was speechless. She had never expected her father to do something like this. She could see that her father felt embarrassed by what he had done. It was only after he had got an erection that he realised that what he was doing to Libby was wrong. She was glad that he stopped and moved away from her and left the room.

Friends in her circle easily led Libby. She wanted to be liked and was influenced by people who took an interest in her. One of the older girls introduced her to a local pimp named Simon. She wasn't aware that he had immediately noticed her vulnerability and had sought deliberately to lure her into his web. Simon belonged to a paedophile ring where Libby was subsequently sold for underage sex. He pocketed the cash whilst Libby was sometimes given presents. She particularly liked a bracelet she had been given and had asked a man who she regularly had sex with to buy her a ring.

She loved the compliments men gave her and relished being told that she was pretty. Libby had told some of her regular clients about her father and how he had touched her breasts. One or two of them pretended that they would pay him a visit and confront him about what he had done and ask him not to do something like that to her ever again. Libby was far too naïve to see the hypocrisy in these statements. Instead, she felt safe that others were willing to keep an eye out for her, and cared enough for her to offer to do these things.

One day, Simon was desperately short of cash to pay off a drug supplier he owed money to. He telephoned Libby and went to greater lengths than usual to praise and charm her.

'You know I've always admired your courage and guts, Libby... especially with you having to live with that father of yours,' he told her.

'Really?' Libby exclaimed in a tone that was looking for more praise and recognition.

On this occasion, after Simon had reiterated his charming charade, he told Libby that he needed her help urgently, to get cash – or else he would be a dead man by teatime that day. The fact that it was she to whom he turned to for help flashed across her mind. She was anxious and upset to hear of his dilemma and wanted to help him. Liking the idea that he considered her as someone special in his life whom he could trust, there was no question of Libby not doing anything Simon asked her to do. She agreed to meet up with him in a café to discuss the plan he had for her in helping him to get the cash.

Whilst drinking a milkshake, Libby was completely absorbed in what he was saying and did not think twice before agreeing to do what was being asked of her. She was given instructions and, despite brief reservations that she might get caught, she agreed to do what Simon asked. She agreed because the last thing she wanted was to disappoint Simon. The mere fact that he thought that she was capable of robbing the bookmakers gave her the confidence that she could carry this off. Simon was never wrong in her eyes in anything he did or said and she trusted him implicitly.

Libby agreed to meet Simon again at a different café two hours later. She then took the knife from him and set off to commit the robbery. But the time came and went and Libby did not return. She had been arrested after her attempt to rob the bookmakers failed to go as planned. Libby was unable to brandish the knife at the cashier in the way Simon had instructed her. She lost her courage and was only able to tell the cashier that she had a knife in her pocket. It was clear that Libby had attempted to do something way out of her league.

The police officers that arrested Libby gave her a severe ticking off. '*Naïve, foolish and irresponsible*' were the words that one of the officers used to describe her. Libby was then taken to the police station for questioning. She was in a state of shock and just sat in the interview room, staring impassively whilst sucking her thumb.

Libby kept thinking about Simon and felt guilty that she would not be able to help him now. She knew that he would still be waiting at the café for her return with the money. Thoughts of him getting murdered for not having the cash later that evening troubled Libby more than the predicament that she had gotten herself into.

As Libby was waiting to sign her bail sheet at the police station she pictured Simon in her mind leaving the café and felt disappointed that she had let him down. What she didn't know then, but would later find out from a friend, was that when she didn't turn up that afternoon with the cash, Simon went to another part of town and sought alternative help for his cash flow difficulties. Libby didn't believe her friend's advice that Simon couldn't care less about her and that thoughts of her were far from his mind. Libby justified his abandonment by thinking that he thought she had deliberately let him down. She decided that she would apologise to Simon the next time they met up. The thoughts of seeing him again excited her and she planned to be a better friend to him the next time he asked her for a favour. Her naïvety even extended beyond her hoping that Simon would accept her explanation and apology for the botched robbery. The circle of deceit was still in full flow. It clearly had some more spins to make before Libby would realise that she had been used. Then, and only then, would the circle be able to come to a halt.

Malena

Malena was obsessed with graffiti and lyric writing. She constantly had a felt-tip pen to hand and used it to scribble her rhymes everywhere she went. She wrote more or less the same thing each time:

> *'Mirror Mirror on the wall*
> *Who's the fairest of them all?*
> *The mirror laughed*
> *And gave a grunt*
> *It sure isn't you*
> *You ugly cunt'*

She wasn't the least bit perturbed when she was given an ASBO* for writing graffiti on various buildings in town. She laughed out loud when she opened the envelope and read out the instructions of the court. Malena decided to pin the court document up alongside posters in her bedroom.

Malena had a daughter who was nearly six-months old. The baby's upbringing was left to Malena's mother who had persuaded her not to have an abortion. She offered to look after the baby whilst Malena continued at school. This was not an easy task as Malena was from a family of six children. There were times when the chaotic overcrowding of the household could only be described as utter mayhem. Malena's father worked very long hours by opting to do overtime at every opportunity – but he still went to the pub after work and would stay there until closing time to avoid the havoc at home.

Malena could not bear to look at her baby and resisted holding her, often remarking how ugly her daughter looked. She chose to stay out late at night with friends and challenged any discipline that her mother attempted to impose. This sometimes entailed her having lengthy arguments with her exhausted mother. She continued at school but this was a matter of just attending, as she was completely

---

*ASBO – Abbreviation for Anti-Social Behaviour Order.

unconcerned about course work or impending exams.

Malena excelled in extraordinary sexualised behaviour whenever she was out with her friends. She had a favourite bench in the main shopping area of town where she would sit smoking with two or three of her friends. They would target young men they fancied and there were several ways that Malena set out to either impress or embarrass them and her friends.

'Hi there… have you got a big dick?' – 'She wants to know,' Malena would then add, pointing to one of her friends.

'Now, tell us which one of you boys has the biggest dick?' she would enquire if there were two or three young males passing at the same time.

More often than not the response from the young men was either laughter or friendly camaraderie. However, there were a few occasions when Malena's questions resulted in her being called abusive names.

Through her crude questioning about the size of male genitalia she made a new friend or, at least, that is what she thought had happened. The young man was about two years older than her. They had become acquainted after seeing each other whenever he passed through town. He used to stop briefly and have a chat but always declined to sit down on the bench with Malena. They didn't really have a proper conversation as their exchange of words mainly consisted of sexual innuendos.

One day when Malena was alone waiting for her friends to arrive he suddenly appeared. This meeting proved to be different. The innuendos increased with the young man testing Malena's defences. She was made to feel that she had to prove that she was as daring with her actions as she was with her pervasive remarks.

Before long she found herself being accompanied down a quiet side street where she consented to have unprotected sex. She felt indifferent about having sex with the young man. But she reasoned it was just sex and something that she could brag about to her friends later.

After they had finished having sex the young man turned to Malena and asked, 'Now does that answer your question?' in relation to her previous questioning on the size of his manhood.

She was never to see him again after that day despite keeping an eye out for him. Looking for sightings of the young man soon faded as fears of being pregnant began to take hold. Her friends asked her what she would do if she was pregnant.

'Probably get rid of it,' she replied.

She tried to push the thoughts to the back of her mind. She hadn't had this problem the first time she got pregnant. Her mother had promptly taken charge of the situation and was thoughtful and reassuring. Malena feared that she would be less supportive this time owing to her being so tired with the heavy workload at home. However, in the meantime, she continued meeting her friends as well as getting up to her usual pranks. Occasionally, she risked the conditions of her ASBO and one day in town she chanced writing her rhyme *'Mirror Mirror…'* on a wall when no one was looking.

Her mother fell ill with a severe chest infection and was confined to bed, causing Malena to receive a sharp reality shock. Her baby was now hungry, crying and needed a nappy change. The kitchen sink was full of dishes and the feeding utensils needed sterilising. Her siblings offered no help and her father refused to take time off work. Malena found herself isolated at home, looking after her baby daughter and attending to her sick mother. Initially, she didn't find looking after the baby simple and had constantly to ask her mother for advice. However, she discovered that there was a part of her that liked this new-found sense of responsibility.

Malena's world was rocked when she found out she really was pregnant. Confusion, turmoil and anger passed through her mind. Even though her pregnancy was in its early stages she felt she had to make a decision fairly rapidly about what she wanted to do. Because of her growing reputation for promiscuous behaviour she had fallen out with many of her friends. There was now only one friend with whom she could confide in and discuss her predicament – and the friend suggested she accompany her to the local medical centre to enquire about a termination.

The counsellor talked through all the various options and gave her some literature to take away and read. She was advised not to rush into a decision. But there was something that clicked in Malena's mind during the meeting where she decided to go ahead with the termination feeling that this option was the most feasible one. Her mind was firmly decided. She put the leaflets the counsellor had given to her in the waste bin outside the medical centre. Malena then asked her friend to take the next day off school as she needed someone to accompany her to the clinic and look after her daughter whilst she was having the termination.

The termination was quick and straightforward. She felt little emotion during the procedure but afterwards wondered if she had done the right thing. These thoughts came instantly the moment she rejoined her friend and baby in the waiting room. She tried to behave normally as she lifted her daughter to cuddle her. Malena didn't feel in the mood for conversation and thankfully her friend didn't ask her questions. She just wanted to leave the building and get away from the place as quickly as possible. Right at that moment she needed space, silence and a cigarette.

Malena continued to be in a low mood for several days afterwards but continued with her usual routine at home. Her mother's chest infection had improved and she was able to get up for longer periods. Having chats with her mother about everyday things brightened her up and she began to think less of the termination. Malena had begun to get along better with her mother whilst she had taken care of her during her illness. Their arguments were fewer and a sense of calmness had begun to creep into their relationship. Malena talked to her mother about returning to school and taking her exams. Despite having an indifferent attitude towards her education she knew that it was better if she continued going to school until after she had taken her exams.

Malena's baby was crawling on the floor as she chatted to her mother. When the baby approached the settee she grabbed hold of Malena's feet. Malena looked down and for the first time ever felt genuine affection for her daughter. She saw magic in her daughter's eyes as they gazed straight at each other. A feeling of pride and tenderness prompted her to pick her baby up and start pretending that she was tickling her. They began to have great fun together with the baby chuckling as she was being bounced. Malena hadn't experienced such delight and enjoyment in ages.

Malena decided she would return to school the following week. Her mother was much improved by this time and Malena was anxious to return and settle down to her studies. Perhaps this turnaround in her behaviour was a glimpse of hopefulness for the future. On the other hand, it may have been just an interlude; only time would tell whether or not she would return to her old ways.

But then neither was it certain that she would return to her previous irresponsible ways. An aura of hope for the future was beginning to appear in her life. Right at that moment this could only be construed as a good thing for Malena and her baby.

Nerissa

One day Nerissa pulled back the lace curtain in her bedroom and looked outside at the orange developing in the sky. The day looked drab but had a stillness about it that suited Nerissa's mood. After a few minutes standing in a daze she realised that she must set her mind to writing the letters that needed to be written. She had made her mind up to kill herself in the coming week – but, as yet, hadn't decided how she was going to do it, hence the delay. Switching on the heater made the window-pane drip with condensation. Looking at this prompted a further delay in writing the letters.

After she had written notes to her brothers and sisters – and Nick, a boy she fancied at school, she began writing a goodbye letter to her parents:

> 'Dear Mum and Dad,
>
> I want you to know how sorry I am writing you this letter. I love you both very much and I am sure that you love me too. I can't cope with the torture they are putting me through anymore. My life has become a total nightmare day and night. I don't want to have to go through it anymore. They tease me unbearably everyday because they hate me so much. No matter what I do or say they find ways of getting to me. There is just no way that I want to carry on like this…'

Nerissa was only halfway through the letter when one of her sisters came into the bedroom. She hadn't expected this and hurriedly pretended that she was doing some homework. Nerissa lived with her two brothers and three sisters in a very small and overcrowded flat. She had to share a bedroom with her sisters, which made the room very cramped. As Nerissa was the eldest child in the family she bore a lot of responsibility in helping her parents raise the younger children. The combined household income failed to cover bills and food expenses. This meant that family meals were often kept to a minimum. Being from a poor family the children were bought few new clothes or shoes and were mainly dressed from charity shops.

Clothes were handed down from the older siblings to the younger ones. Luxuries were non-existent and the family had never been able to afford a holiday. However, they enjoyed Christmases together and Nerissa always enjoyed the fun and friendship with her brothers and sisters at times like this. Overall, she was quite close to all her family, which was a good thing because she was unable to make many friends outside home because of her shyness. But she really liked Nick at school and imagined them to be madly in love with each other. Fantasising about Nick often made her imagine writing Christmas cards with her signing both their names on them. However, she had never spoken to Nick and realised deep down that it was unlikely he even noticed her when they passed each other in the corridors at school.

Nerissa stood out from the other young people at school. Apart from wearing an old brown overcoat with a fur collar over her school uniform, she stood out from the other girls in her class because she was more academically gifted. They knew that she would inevitably get better exam results than they would and this made them very envious – and therefore they set out to undermine her whenever an opportunity arose.

A group of girls in the same class as Nerissa, and one girl in particular, Scarlet, did their best to make Nerissa's life unbearable. Scarlet was small in stature and would squirm up her face into a fake smile every time she saw Nerissa. She was the epitome of sarcasm.

'Oh, what a lovely coat you are wearing today,' Scarlet would say to Nerissa – adding with a sting in her voice 'Did you borrow it from your grandmother?'

Nerissa never made any reply to the daily taunts.

The other girls would think this hilarious and begin to laugh at Nerissa and taunt her. Even though Nerissa hated her coat and was deeply embarrassed by it, it was wintertime and she had nothing else to wear. After nearly a year of persistent teasing, she could take no more. At lunch time one day she went to get her lunch box from her locker. Scarlet and the others were in the locker room as well and when they saw Nerissa enter they nudged each other.

'Have you come to get your scraps for lunch… you poor hungry little puppy?' Scarlet promptly piped up.

She then moved closer to Nerissa and peeped into her lunch box.

'Oh, girls, it's a leftover pork pie that she's got for lunch… how delicious,' she sarcastically continued.

Nerissa felt anger swelling up within her but managed not to utter a word. The bitchy remarks continued. Something snapped inside Nerissa's head as she turned around and swung her hand to strike Scarlet forcefully across the face. Scarlet slumped backwards in a vain attempt to dodge the slap but instead fell against a row of lockers. The noise of the impact frightened Nerissa and for a couple of moments she felt remorse for what she had done. She even momentarily considered making an apology but these thoughts were eclipsed by Scarlet's retort.

'You bloody lunatic! You are a lunatic as well as being a bloody odd ball!' she screamed at Nerissa.

The other girls then joined in and made similar remarks. But the sudden rush of adrenaline prompted Nerissa to answer back without hesitation.

'You got what you deserved and will get another slap if you do not stop bothering me with your nonsense,' she assertively exclaimed back to Scarlet.

Although these words were expressed in a reasonably calm manner, Nerissa was trembling all over. This was the only occasion that she had instinctively been able to respond to the bullying. She had hoped that things would change and that some of the teasing would stop after this, but this was not to be. Instead, things continued as usual and she again drew back into herself, unable to respond to their insults and nasty remarks. If anything, her tormentors increased their level of bullying. They did things to her in classes when the teacher's attention had been distracted. On the face of it, none of it was terribly serious. For example, Scarlet put a large amount of salt in a chicken curry that

Nerissa was helping to cook. Little tricks like this were pushing her into greater despair, making her mind dwell on the possibility of suicide. She began to picture a date and how she would do it.

A week later though something wonderful happened that almost made Nerissa pinch herself with disbelief. She heard some unexpected good news about Scarlet and her family moving away from the area. Nerissa couldn't believe it and wondered was it for real or just wishful thinking – casting her attention to happy endings she had read in storybooks.

But the realisation of Scarlet moving away became a reality. The other bullies became less of an influence after her departure. They gradually lost interest in mocking and taunting Nerissa and in the end they totally left her alone. Nerissa got her life back. It was almost as if someone had stolen it and suddenly the thieves had been apprehended.

Nerissa destroyed all her goodbye notes that she had written except the one she had penned to Nick. This was more of a love note than anything else. Getting up and going to school was no longer the agony that it used to be. In fact it became a bit of a delight, especially on the days that she saw Nick. Nerissa's sister in whom she had confided was encouraging her to speak to him, or at the very least to smile so as to test his reaction.

It was no surprise that Nerissa passed all her exams with high grades whilst her former tormentors only achieved moderate ones. She could now see light at the end of the tunnel. Her self-confidence began to increase as the trauma of the nightmare she endured started to subside. She was now free to plan her future. A future that held much promise and potential now that the torture she had endured for so long had come to an end. Maybe this bright future might contain Nick but if it didn't, she was almost sure that she would find someone equally as alluring – with her new-found sense of self worth and purpose.

Olga

Olga loved songs and music. She had no preference provided she could dance to its rhythm. She was fascinated by a piece that she had learned in drama classes at school. It went like this:

Growing up in Galway,
Is the perfect place to be,
Without a care in the world,
You can set your troubles free

She clapped and danced with joy as the last lines reached a high octave. Olga loved the routine of school and enjoyed learning a variety of subjects. Her school attendance in Bosnia was erratic but she relished going to school in Ireland. It was a big mixed school and she took great delight in wearing her new school uniform.

Olga came from a Bosnian gypsy community. She was bonded to her family and culture and had a sense of duty towards both. This attachment did not change when she came to Ireland. She mixed mainly with relatives and friends who shared her heritage and experiences. Olga had suffered terribly as a child and was forced to flee when Bosnian warlords began targeting her community. The police, too, were known to often deliver horrific beatings to people who did not cooperate. But in Galway the *gardai* never bothered Olga's family. She was suspicious of them at first but then she noticed how friendly they appeared to be.

Olga and her family were housed in the suburban part of the city and were generally pleased with their home. They were close to both the city and countryside. Their neighbours were friendly but the language deterred Olga from making many friends, hence closeness remained with her own community. Although her written English was moderately good, she was still in need of verbal improvement in the language.

Olga enjoyed going for trips in her uncle's van around the local countryside. She liked seeing the occasional Irish travelling family who had taken up temporary residence along the roadside on the outskirts of Galway. She compared these scenes to aspects of her culture in Bosnia. Often when passing one of these caravan sites she would wave to the children who were playing outside. She loved it when they waved back.

Olga did not have any goals in her life and had never really thought about her future. She feared that this might entail having to return to Bosnia, so she put it to the back of her mind. At that moment she was enjoying school and appreciated learning new ways and absorbing information that made life more interesting.

But Olga's life was to suddenly take a dramatic turn. Events happened so fast that she didn't properly understand either the short or long term implications of her actions. When Olga was taken to the *garda* station for questioning, she was at a loss to understand the fuss. At first she thought it was an immigration interview and feared deportation back to Bosnia. Olga had become friendly with older teenagers and her new so-called friends had taken advantage of her naivety. Olga was innocent to the rules and laws of her new country but this was about to change with a harsh lesson in what happens to someone who doesn't abide by the law.

Just a few days before the incident occurred, Olga couldn't believe her luck when some girls in her class began to be friendlier to her than usual. Until then, she had found it difficult to fit in. Now she readily joined them and tried her best to blend in with their jokes and humour. Unfortunately, she wasn't astute enough to recognise the innuendoes that came her way. She was oblivious that her new friends were laughing and joking with her in a condescending way or that their imitations of her accent bore malice and she was being used as the butt of their jokes.

Olga was delighted when her friends suggested that they all meet up in the city centre for a general outing. The city was a hub of activity and they had only been together for less than half an hour when one of the girls in the group found a lost wallet with a credit card in it –

along with the pin number. Olga had never seen a credit card before and had to ask her friends what it was. They explained what it was and how the pin number worked. Olga laughed and referred to it as a 'magic card'. Her friends dared her to go into an electrical shop and buy a camcorder that was on display in the window. She did this and to their surprise, she got away with it. Olga was next accompanied to an off licence to buy some alcohol but on this occasion she came unstuck. She presented the credit card when attempting to buy two bottles of gin. The shop assistant became suspicious of Olga and asked for further identification. Olga said she didn't have any. Within a few minutes *gardai* arrived on the scene.

Olga was scared, lonely and frightened in the *garda* station. She had answered all the questions honestly and truthfully because she did not consider her actions to be wrong. She believed she was out with her friends and that what they were doing was only a little fun, which wasn't causing harm to anyone. But she was in for a bit of a surprise when the station sergeant told Olga that she might have destroyed her chances and those of her family of gaining asylum in Ireland – as a result of her having been charged with forgery and deception. Olga's mother, who was present for the interview, began shouting at her in Bosnian. Eventually her bail was set and she was freed from custody. She cried all the way home as it began to sink in what might happen in the months to come.

The other girls with Olga that day had fled the scene before the *gardai* had arrived. They were never caught because Olga refused to divulge their names to the *gardai*. She considered that this would have been a disloyal thing to do, especially as she hated the thought of their mothers being angry with them too.

Olga was silent on the way home from the police station. She could not even hum her favourite rhythm. The words came into her head but she kept trying to shut them out: *Growing up in Galway, Is the perfect place to be, Without a care in the world, You can set your troubles free…* as they continued going round and round in her head.

Olga's family continued to be angry with her in the days and weeks that followed. She was often subjected to long periods of silence. Attending school provided some reprieve from her family's anger – but she was saddened that the girls whom she had temporarily considered her friends would no longer speak to her. The concept of taking each day at a time had taken on a whole new meaning and it was far from being a pleasant feeling.

Olga had become accustomed to taking each day as it came in Bosnia. Now she found herself doing the same in Ireland. But the future didn't appear to have any silver lining. Now she was in a position where it wasn't possible to dream of a new beginning in a faraway land – like she had done in her darkest moments in Bosnia. Her faraway land had become a reality. Now she was in Ireland and, because of a mistake she had made, she dreaded that she and her family may have to return to their previous existence of fear and torture.

Philip

Philip knew he had a supportive foster parent in Michelle Parker. He had lived with Michelle for nearly a year. Philip was able to confide in Michelle and they had developed a trusting relationship. He let her know that his ex-girlfriend had given birth to a baby son nearly a year previously but that her parents wouldn't allow him to have contact with her or their baby any more. Philip spoke candidly about how his ex-girlfriend's parents thought he was a bad influence on their daughter because of his drinking reputation, drug taking and involvement in criminal activities. Whilst it was true that he had done all of these things and had been in trouble several times with the police, he had, however, calmed down a lot since going into foster care.

Philip had told Michelle all about the tough time he had as a young boy. His parents separated when he was five and he went to live with his father. His father was a heavy drinker and became extremely violent when drunk – often turning his anger towards Philip. His mother, on the other hand, had a serious drug addiction and was imprisoned for drug dealing when he was seven.

Philip really wanted to see his baby son and had talked this through with Michelle. He was drinking far less than usual and hardly smoked cannabis any more. He had also, under the guidance of Michelle, approached various colleges for their prospectuses and he was showing an interest in becoming a plumber or an electrician.

Philip asked Michelle to accompany him around to his ex-girlfriend's house to see his baby. It was soon be his son's first birthday. They planned the visit in advance. Philip was encouraged by Michelle to write to his ex-girlfriend's father – Mr Baker – to inform him how he was planning to go to college to learn an apprenticeship. This would show how Philip was changing his ways for the better. Philip didn't receive a reply to his letter and therefore assumed that it would be alright for him to visit. He went out shopping and bought a lovely black and white panda bear to take as a present to his son.

The welcome at the Baker household didn't go as expected. Philip was door-stepped by Mr Baker and wasn't invited into the house. There was more to the unfriendly manner that greeted Philip and Michelle. Despite telling Mr Baker that he had turned over a new leaf and hadn't touched drink or drugs in the previous six months, he was still met with animosity. Philip could clearly see this in the facial expression of Mr Baker. He got upset by this and started demanding to see his baby.

'I just want to see him… just give me five minutes with him please… I got him a present,' he pleaded to Mr Baker.

'No way are you going to enter this house,' Mr Baker abruptly answered.

'Why not?' Philip countered.

'Look, you are not going to have anything else ever to do with this family… leopards don't change their spots… you have caused nothing but trouble to my family… you little thug,' Mr Baker told Philip in an aggressive tone and then closed the door. Philip walked away and was completely crestfallen. He felt worthless and could never imagine a time when he would be allowed to see his son. He was unable to pay much attention to Michelle's comforting words telling him that Mr Baker needed some more time to calm down and stop being angry with him.

That night Philip was completely restless and went out and met up with some friends. One of his friends managed to get hold of some vodka, rum and beer at an off licence and they went off into a local park. It was a lovely summer's evening and Philip was determined to get drunk so that he could forget about his day. One thing led to another and then a hasty plan was put into action to burgle a jewellery shop in town.

All the young people in the group were willing to participate in the burglary. Philip volunteered to use a metal bar to break a back window to get into the shop. They knew they had to be quick because they feared an alarm might go off. Luckily for them it did not. Philip and his accomplices managed to steal several watches and chains. Suddenly, he heard a loud noise. The sharp thought of getting caught sobered his drunken state. It was a false alarm though. The noise outside turned out to be a man starting up his motorbike. Philip's peace of mind was restored after the man had ridden off.

Philip realised that their fingerprints would be found in the shop. He and his friends wiped some of the surfaces they had touched with their sleeves but Philip was still undecided whether this was enough to cover up any forensic evidence and decided to set fire to the shop by lighting some paper in a nearby rubbish bin. Philip and his accomplices then fled the scene as speedily as they could.

When Philip got home he sat at the side of his bed and looked at some of the watches he had stolen. What had seemed a great idea an hour previously was less so after the excitement had worn off. He thought to himself how foolish he had been and regretted what he had done.

The days passed by and Philip lived constantly in fear of being caught for burglary and arson. He was fidgety the whole time and when Michelle asked him what was wrong he just shrugged his shoulders and pretended that the disappointment of not been allowed to see his son was responsible for his sulky mood. Listening to Michelle talking about starting college did not interest him in the least. Suggestions that he could go to see a solicitor to enquire about his legal rights in relation to contact with his son scared him. This really made him nervous, as he could not bear contact with anyone in a legal role.

'If you don't tell me what's going on in your head, I can't help you,' Michelle said to Philip in an exasperated tone.

'Just leave me alone,' he shouted back at Michelle before walking out of the house.

The thought of him ever being allowed to see and hold his baby did not seem real. He was even beginning to think that this was for the best as he began to consider that he would not make a good father. Fear of getting caught for the robbery and the fire were at the forefront of his thoughts and shaded all his previous worries. Feeling awful he decided that he would go to a friend's place and bury his feelings of despair with some drink.

The alcohol made Philip settle down a little. He began to feel less stressed and started to consider his options, although his thoughts were racing through all the various possibilities. He began to consider whether it would be best to tell Michelle about the robbery. Maybe she could advise him about what was the best thing to do – but then it was difficult to gauge her possible reaction. Michelle might throw him out of the house and then report him to the police. On the other hand she might suggest accompanying him to the police station. If that was the case would it not be better if he handed himself over to the police himself without involving Michelle? However, knowing that he would probably get custody if he confessed didn't warm him too kindly to this idea for very long.

The only other alternative was to carry on as if nothing had happened and hope that he wouldn't get caught – and even if he was brought in for questioning the choice of denying involvement was a viable preference to admitting guilt. Confusion ensued and Philip ended the evening at his friend's house feeling more wretched and fed up with his life than he had been at the beginning. He cursed the alcohol for not helping him.

Feeling inebriated he decided that the only thing he wanted to do then was to go home and sleep. At least this would provide refuge for a few hours from the painfully confusing thoughts. He didn't want to think any more about anything because none of the questions he asked himself provided any answers. Sleep would at least be an escape from his predicament until the next day. But even in his intoxicated state he knew that when the next day arrived he would have to face the reality of his life all over again.

The reality of life can be pleasant or unpleasant but either way it is resolute in never going away. Before Philip left his friend's house he placed his hands over his head. He would have preferred nothing more than to have come up with a solution that would have fixed all his worries. But the solution wasn't forthcoming. Perhaps, the next day, or one of those that followed, would be kinder to him, providing him with the answers that he sought.

Quin

Quin had a fascination with death. In fact it was more than a fascination since he liked to dwell on the topic in conversations with friends and would ask them their views on death and dying. Quin could not understand how characters on television were one moment alive and talking and the next thing their heads would just flop back and they'd be dead. He wondered what they had seen and how they felt when they died. He thought it was really lousy that people died and never came back to life again.

Home life for Quin was a living hell and had been throughout his short life. His father was a heavy drinker who physically abused Quin's mother almost on a daily basis in front of him. Because of this, he had been taken into care but had been allowed back home when the situation appeared to have improved. This improvement was short lived and it was not long before his father began drinking again and violence continued at home.

Quin then ran away. He slept rough in parks in a nearby town but the police found him and took him home. His mother persuaded him to stay and told him that she needed him as a support against his father. This request from his mother made Quin feel valued and boosted his confidence. He even decided that the next time he saw his father strike out at his mother, he would go to her defence and challenge him. Sadly, this did not go according to plan. Quin did challenge his father on the next beating but received an almighty battering himself for interfering in what his father described as 'none of his concern'. Quin endured heavy bruising in the assault and also suffered an injured back. He decided to run away again but opted this time to put a greater distance between him and his home town.

Quin got off the train at Charing Cross and wandered into Leicester Square. He kept walking along the pavements fascinated by the busy environment. Quin politely enquired directions to Piccadilly Circus from a passer by. He had heard that there were organisations in this area where nice people would help him with his problems. During the train journey, he had prepared in his mind what he would tell them about his father. He would also ask them for help for his mother.

Quin found Piccadilly Circus to be a place full of life and activity. He couldn't stop staring at the illuminations. A Japanese tourist stood close to him and was taking pictures of buses on a digital camera. Quin wondered why he was doing this. He had never seen anyone in his home town take a picture of a bus before. He thought this a rather odd thing to do.

Then suddenly another man was standing beside Quin. The man looked and smiled at Quin and asked him his name before enquiring if he was lost. Quin instantly thought that he was one of these nice people that helped others. He started telling the man why he had come to London. He was a little embarrassed though and only managed to tell him that he had run away from home after getting beaten up by his father. He had the bruises to prove it. The man kept on smiling and reassured Quin that he was safe now. He suggested that they go to a nearby café on Brewer Street for something to eat and drink.

Quin felt more comfortable in the café and opened up more to the man about his difficulties. The man suggested that he come and stay the night at his flat until he got himself sorted out with accommodation. He added that he knew of places that Quin could go to the next day where he could get fixed up with a place to stay and where food would be provided. This all sounded good to Quin as he had little money left after the train journey.

When they got to the man's flat, Quin was offered a beer but he declined. He said he would prefer a glass of orange juice instead. They watched television for a bit and then a DVD.

Quin was invited into the kitchen to help fix supper. He was quite relaxed at this stage and it was nice and warm in the flat. He felt tired and was looking forward to having a good sleep. Whilst Quin was sitting at the table eating, the man brushed alongside him and kissed him on the top of the head. Next thing, he was on his knees unzipping Quin's trousers and taking out his penis. Quin flinched and then froze in his seat as the man started performing oral sex. When the sensation of ejaculation came to Quin, he suddenly jumped up from his seat. The man did not expect this to happen and slumped forward on the floor. He instantly got very angry at Quin and shouted:

'What did you do that for?' before adding 'I think it's time you went to bed – now!' placing emphasis on the word 'now'.

When Quin got up the next morning the man was cheerful and made him some breakfast. He also had some addresses written out for him to go to for help with accommodation. Quin remained quiet. He no longer trusted the man but took the note with the addresses as well as accepting a small amount of money for bus fares back to the West End.

Whilst Quin was waiting at the bus stop he looked at the piece of paper the man had given him and wondered if it was a trick for him to go to other places where he would be made to do more dirty things. This prompted him to screw the paper up in a ball. Quin felt miserable and wondered if he was responsible for the man's perversion by having said or done something.

Feelings of bewilderment and loneliness crowded over Quin. His trust had been betrayed and he had feelings of emptiness. He was completely unsure about what he should do. It was less than twenty-four hours since he had run away from home and things had turned out so unfortunate for him. There was no way, he thought to himself, that he could have had any inkling that things could get so awful. It's not that he treated coming to London as a big adventure. He just wanted to get away from his violent father. But now he was in a big city that had provided new fears and which scared him in a different way. Quin definitely had no desire to return home but was gradually growing unsure as to whether London was the best place for him. But then where else, he asked himself, could he go?

Quin got off the bus in Piccadilly and walked aimlessly up the street until he came to a church within a courtyard. The church clock was chiming. Quin looked up at the bell tower and was fascinated by the beautiful sound of the chimes. It was exactly eleven o'clock. He decided to go into the courtyard of the church and sit on one of the benches and rest for a while. It was a lovely sunny day and it felt calm and peaceful there despite the busy traffic and hustle and bustle outside.

A lady approached Quin and introduced herself as a representative from the church. He was nervous and timidly responded to her questions. Reluctant to do much talking at first, he gradually began to respond better after he saw how caring and nice she appeared to be. Parts of her demeanour reminded him of his mother. He accepted her invitation to join her for something to eat in a caravan stationed on the opposite side of the courtyard. After he was given a cup of tea and some biscuits Quin told the woman the reasons why he had come to London. Responding to the rapport that he was building up with her he told her all about the violence at home and how he never wanted to return. Sadness was etched on his face when he told the lady that he missed his mum, brothers and sisters.

Then Quin suddenly burst into tears. He began sobbing his heart out when telling the lady about the awful thing the man had done to him the night before. The woman gave reassurance to Quin that what had happened wasn't his fault and told him that she would be willing to go along with him to the police station to report the assault. The mention of the police prompted Quin to plead with the woman not to involve the law because he felt they would make him go back home and that was the last thing he wanted to happen. After being assured that this would not happen, Quin was told that he would be given help to avoid returning home, for the time being at least.

Quin began to brighten up and felt better after it was explained to him that he would not be placed under pressure to do anything he didn't want to do. He sat back in his seat and relaxed his feet. A timid smile crept across his face when he asked the lady if he could have another one of her biscuits. He felt safe and since it was a feeling that he hadn't experienced in a long time, another biscuit added to the delight of the moment. In fact, he gladly accepted two more biscuits that were given to him.

Ruby

'You lot are all the fucking same… fucking wankers,' screamed Ruby as she was being arrested.

Ruby had a reputation in her neighbourhood as someone not to be messed around with. Her friends were terrified of her. 'You're all pussies… stop being scared shitless,' she would tell them. She considered herself the leader of the local gang. Together she and the others taunted people in the area with abuse. They had also escaped getting caught before despite having committed several street muggings.

Ruby had deliberately sought out a replica firearm so that she could rob a service station. Her victim was totally traumatised believing the replica gun that Ruby had pointed at her was a real gun.

'The fucking bitch knew it wasn't a real gun,' Ruby retorted after getting arrested at the scene of the crime – before yelling over to her victim 'Stop staring at me you bitch.'

The custody sergeant started to explain to Ruby the procedure of her detention but she interrupted him before he could finish his sentence.

'You lot play psychological games… fucking wankers… pigs… wankers… pigs… I know my rights… so get out of my face, wanker, and get me my solicitor,' she blurted out to the sergeant.

Ruby was put in a cell to cool down, but she was soon banging on the door.

'Get me my solicitor now… wanker,' she screamed. 'You cannot lock me up like this… I need help… I suffer from Sch… Zo… what do you call that word? I need to see a shrink,' she continued.

The claim of suffering from schizophrenia was a fabrication. One of her friends had once told her that 'if you get nicked by the old Bill… you should tell them you are a nutter… demand to see a shrink… and then pretend you are fucking bonkers… my friend's father did this and was let off.'

But telling the police this hadn't provoked the reaction that Ruby expected. Apart from them informing her that a doctor would examine her in due course, they subsequently ignored anything else she had to say. The police were exasperated with her tirade of abuse. Even Ruby was beginning to feel tired of her brawling behaviour and decided to take a rest, but not before she had yelled out, 'Oh go and fuck yourselves,' to the officers assigned to her case.

Ruby was used to making threats or being obnoxious to people. She hated her stepfather and used to call him the most horrific names imaginable. Her mother had remarried twice but had hoped that Ruby would like her third husband. This was not to be as Ruby had a reserve of animosity. She never forgave her mother for leaving her father. She also felt that her mother never paid her enough attention or recognition. Her new stepfather sometimes ignored Ruby's aggressiveness; whilst at other times responded by attempting to impose discipline on her, to little avail. Both her mother and stepfather had thought that a family holiday in Jamaica would help settle Ruby. They were wrong. The holiday was a disaster as Ruby continued to be argumentative and spiteful throughout the vacation.

The inside of the police cell was far removed from the beauty of Jamaica. She smelt at once the accumulated stench of vomit and urine from the previous inhabitants. Her solicitor came and told her that it was unlikely that he would be able to do anything to help her – and was in fact quite frank with her by pointing out that she had been arrested for a very serious offence and that it would be unlikely for bail to be granted. She argued with him to do his best to get her bail. However, later that evening Ruby was charged with attempted robbery with the use of a replica firearm – and was told that she was going to be remanded in custody. Predictably, she flew into another rage, with her solicitor bearing the brunt of her fury.

'Fuck off… wanker… you don't care about me as long as you get paid your cash… fucking wanker… I'll get out of here without your help… now fuck off out of my face… I'm not listening to you wanker… fuck off… go wank yourself,' screamed Ruby at the top of her lungs.

This time she had been caught and there was no way of escaping her wrongdoing. But Ruby was adamant that she would endeavour to make as many attempts as possible to escape responsibility. She was in full victim mode when two police officers approached to take her back to the cell.

'You lot won't get me… I am innocent… stay away from me, wankers… I am not going anywhere… you will have to haul me away – you fucking pricks,' she announced as she spat at the officers.

After she had calmed down Ruby was allowed to telephone her mother. However, she didn't remain composed for very long. She hated listening to criticism and responded at her earliest opportunity in her well-rehearsed venomous way:

'What do you fucking mean… my mess… it's your entire fucking fault… you did this to me,' Ruby quickly retorted to her mother.

'No I didn't, you did this to yourself… how can you turn around and blame me for what you did?' her mother sternly replied.

'You fucking bitch, you never cared about me; I mean nothing to you,' Ruby screamed back to her mother.

The accusations from Ruby to her mother continued going round and round. Silence descended at the other end. Her mother had had enough of Ruby's self-pitying abusiveness and hung up the receiver. There was simply no way that her mother could get through to Ruby when she was this angry. But then, on the other hand, Ruby was no longer respectful towards her mother. Furthermore, she no longer ever had a conversation with anyone that did not involve screaming or abusiveness. This was how she had learned to respond and couldn't see anything wrong with her chosen behaviour.

Life had become completely shaded in red for Ruby. She had grown so used to espousing anger and blame. These emotions had multiplied and multiplied in every corner of her life. Ruby had finessed this art: an art which required for her, no further lessons. After the telephone call to her mother, Ruby decided it was time to find a new target. With this in mind she began banging yet again on her cell door. She wasn't going to wait patiently lest the police officers forget about her. They were being promptly summoned to her and they'd better have earmuffs because she was about to provide them with another dramatic outburst of her finest expletives!

Scott

It was a misty evening in Dublin. *Met Eireann** had forecast heavy rain but this had not materialised. Scott crossed over O'Connell's Bridge and made his way towards Grafton Street. This was his favourite begging spot. He preferred it to other parts of the city because he felt safer here and attracted less attention to himself. Scott was a quiet young man who never responded when people called him abusive names when begging. Neither was he deceitful. An acquaintance once told him that he should display a cardboard sign when out begging that would read, '*Hungry and Homeless*'. When Scott heard this he instantly thought 'but I'm not homeless'. Indeed, although he was hungry he considered that most people get hungry every day and thought that people would laugh at him for being so foolish if he displayed this on a card.

Scott was having a good day. He had nearly matched the monetary target that his father had set. It was approaching Christmas and his father expected him to collect more money than usual as it was generally felt that people were more generous at this time of year.

Scott liked Christmas. It wasn't because he got presents or had a good time at home as this wasn't part of his life. It was just that he reached his father's targets more easily than in the summer time.

Scott was terrorised by his father and endured heavy beatings if he returned home without enough money. Despite pleas that he had tried his best to collect as much as he could, his father used to beat him repeatedly with a leather belt over his back and legs. His father was an alcoholic and relied on Scott to provide the income to pay for his drink. Scott always tried his best to match his father's targets and on the days that he did he would receive much praise.

'Ah, you're a good son, lad,' his father would say to him before giving him a hug.

He would then return a small amount to Scott, to keep for himself. However, Scott would not spend it but, instead, would put it towards

Met Eireann – Irish National Meteorological Service

the next day's target.

Scott lived in an inner-city flat with his father and younger brother. His mother, too, was an alcoholic but lived apart from the family. Scott used to see her from time to time on Grafton Street. She would make all sorts of promises to him. She said that she would stop drinking, get a flat and that he and his younger brother could both come and live with her. Alas, the promises were never fulfilled because they were made whilst under the influence of alcohol. In the end, Scott stopped believing her anyway.

Scott was a regular visitor to Saint Ann's Church in Dawson Street. He found the staff in the tearoom warm and welcoming. Their friendly approach made him feel at ease and they often jokingly enquired if he had a girlfriend. There was a female member of staff that Scott built up a strong rapport with to the point where he felt able to divulge some of his personal circumstances to her about his home life. The woman told Scott that she would have a word with Dave, a social worker attached to the church. The woman did this and Dave agreed to talk to Scott to see if he could help him in any way. He lent a supportive ear to Scott and empathised with him over the difficult situation with his father. Dave encouraged Scott to tell his father how he felt, particularly with regards to begging and wanting to stop. Scott shook his head when Dave said this, as he knew in his heart that it would never work. He knew how his father's mind worked and was able to visualise the type of reaction his father would have in this sort of situation. His feelings for his father were a combination of love and hate all rolled into one.

In what Scott would later consider as a moment of absolute insanity – he agreed to Dave accompanying him home so that he could advocate on his behalf with his father. Admittedly, Scott's father was neither rude nor threatening to Dave. On the other hand, however, he would not admit that Scott was out on the streets begging on his behalf. He then sighed and said that Scott was old enough to make up his own mind and that what he was doing was something that he wanted to do. Furthermore, he denied he was sometimes hard on

Scott and feebly tried to make a joke about a father's duty to keep a son in check, especially since he was a single father.

'It's not easy bringing up two children single handed... that bitch of a wife left me in the lurch, high and dry,' he told Dave.

The glib utterances continued and the conversation went round in circles. Dave knew that he was getting nowhere and decided that it was time to leave. As he was leaving, he said that he would come back again another day.

Dave's attempts to help Scott by going around to the flat failed. The beating that Scott endured that night was perhaps the worst ever. His father savagely beat him with the leather belt over his back, buttocks and legs. He felt that Scott had brought shame on him by bringing in outside help. Scott was left shaking for hours afterwards from the shock of the ferocious attack. This was gradually replaced with pain.

Dave was true to his word and called around to the flat again, but when he knocked on the door, Scott's father yelled loudly from a window telling him that he wasn't welcome. As a result there were no more visits either from Dave or indeed any other social worker. More poignantly, there were no more trips to Saint Ann's Church for Scott. The fear of upsetting his father again put a halt to this, because the emotional fear was far more painful than any actual beating.

Scott continued his daily begging sessions on Grafton Street. There he could be found walking up and down the street or sometimes sitting down on the pavement asking people for spare change. He remained as meticulous as ever at reaching his father's targets. Scott blocked out thinking about the future, deciding instead to concentrate on the day-to-day tasks of pleasing his father.

Scott's sensitivity and inner beauty hadn't turned into bitterness but his dreams for a bright future had begun to dim over time as his child-hood days were beginning to ebb away. Perhaps a pendulum of change would eventually descend upon him as he begged on the streets. Maybe he might even realise that he deserved a better life than the one he had got – and would one day go on to receive the recognition he deserved for being such a fine person.

Todd

Todd and the other players were all breathless, tired and sweaty after football practice. As always, Todd hurriedly showered and changed because he felt uncomfortable lingering in the changing rooms for longer than was necessary. The main reason for this was because he hated having to keep up the pretence in front of his friends. He found the changing rooms a breeding ground for teasing about girls and who fancied whom. Wisecracks were exchanged about who had big 'tits' and who had small ones. And, of course, there was the usual mixture of lies and truth about relationships at their school.

Todd was able to sometimes join in and make comments to his male friends. He was friendly with some girls and knew things to say to his male peers to avoid detection or, at least, this was how he felt. But he still remained sceptical to whether they suspected him or not. He felt they sometimes stared at him without reason but then, on the other hand, nobody had ever said anything to his face that would have questioned his sexual orientation.

Todd had known Mark for nearly a year and had fancied him from the moment he laid eyes on him. He thought he was the best-looking male he had ever met. His infatuation grew over time, especially after they had become friends. Everything about Mark interested and fascinated him. The words he used, his handwriting, clothes, watch and earring. But most of all he adored Mark's brown eyes.

So greatly was Todd impressed with Mark that he listened attentively to everything he said and usually agreed with his point of view. He was intrigued that Mark had stolen a watch. The fact that Mark had been caught for this and had a court case pending did not detract from the admiration he felt. Todd even tried to steal one himself by going into a department store but could not muster up enough mettle to carry out the theft. However, he promised himself that he would try again and hoped to be triumphant on the second attempt. He thought it would be a nice way to impress Mark if he was successful.

A new football coach had set up a local team aimed at getting young people interested in sports. This was intended as a deterrent to get young people away from anti-social behaviour and the emerging drug culture of the surrounding neighbourhoods. Todd only joined the football team because Mark was interested, but his mild interest in the game increased as time passed until finally he proved himself to be a reasonably good player and was given recognition by other players on the team.

As well as the uncomfortable feelings that Todd endured in the changing rooms he also returned to an atmosphere of discord at home. He lived with his father and three siblings. His mother had died when he was a young child. Todd did not get along with his older sister and constantly bickered with her. Todd's sister accused him of spending too long in the bathroom and often jokingly asked him if he wanted to borrow her make-up kit. This embarrassed Todd, especially when she said it in front of his father and younger brothers who used to burst out laughing. He particularly disliked the attention this drew to him, as he didn't want the others to consider he had feminine traits. Todd often swore at his sister and would shout 'Piss off' to her. He would only stop shouting after his father told him to calm down.

Todd's father had a strict, humourless personality, though he was a good provider for his children and was usually generous with pocket money. But his cold exterior covered a reckless streak, and Todd was fully aware of this. He often gambled large amounts of money on the horses; sometimes losing all his bets whilst at other times winning large amounts of money.

It was the way that Todd's father viewed the world that revealed his most attractive traits. Todd heard him use a term constantly in conversation when referring to certain individuals or groups in society: the words *'not normal'* were used to describe just about everything ranging from mixed-race marriages to women bus drivers. He attributed this description to anyone or anything that met with his disapproval. Needless to say, gay people did not escape his discriminatory attitudes. Todd repeatedly listened to his father's prejudices but usually tried shutting his mind off to what he was hearing.

Todd

Todd's team were meeting for a final practice before the match the coming Saturday. The match itself was to be a friendly game with another team from a neighbouring town, but nevertheless Todd and his team-mates wanted to win and knew they would have to put extra effort into their practice to avoid being beaten. The football pitch was wet after recent heavy rain and Todd found it a hard struggle when chasing the ball and this resulted in him slipping several times. It didn't help either, that the coach bellowed out instructions which put him in a bad mood. He thought his skill and speed were good and did not appreciate being berated.

Todd was close to the goal area, waiting for Mark to pass him the ball, when another player came from behind. During an abrupt tackle Mark tripped and fell to the ground. Todd went over and tried to help him up. He could see that Mark had an injured ankle making it impossible for him to stand. Todd placed his hand on his shoulder and reassured him that it would be okay. This was the first time that Todd had prolonged physical contact with Mark – and this experience proved different to anything he had ever felt before. His feelings were inexplicable and defied description but had a profound effect that deepened his love for Mark.

Mark was taken to hospital for an x-ray and Todd went home alone – alone in the sense that he had no-one to turn to for solace. His inner confusion and anguish had to be borne inwardly in the absence of having someone close to him in whom he could confide his feelings.

When Saturday came Todd was anxious to get the match over with as Mark was not playing because the x-ray showed a fracture. However, Todd was pleased to see that he had come along to the match to support the team. Playing in the match without Mark was torture for Todd. He could not concentrate properly and kept glancing up to the spectators' stand to see him. Todd scored a goal in the first half of the game that equalised the teams. But in the second half it began to rain heavily and just before full time the opponents scored another goal, which meant that the home team had to concede defeat.

Todd wasn't too bothered about losing the match. All he wanted to do was to get out of the rain and change into dry clothes. Then something happened that would transform his life. He ignored the bravado and analysis of the match amongst the players in the changing room. Todd said goodbye to his fellow players with the excuse that he had to rush off to meet his father and sister in town. He closed the changing room door and was heading towards the exit when he bumped into Mark. He was surprised to see him as he thought he had already gone home. Mark made some remark about them losing the match and gave Todd a hug as a consoling gesture. It was at this moment that Todd suddenly and unexpectedly gave Mark a kiss on the cheek. The kiss was quick and fleeting and as soon as he had done it, he hurriedly left the building without any further talk to Mark.

When he returned home his father was engrossed in a newspaper article and muttered some bigoted words about something that met with his disapproval. Todd heard the usual words *'not normal'* as he closed his bedroom door. He lay on his bed. Feelings of elation and regret flashed through his mind. One part of him thought kissing Mark was a huge mistake and the other part felt quite pleased. He did fear some possible repercussions though and imagined things that others might say about him if they found out. His imagination was running wild with various possibilities as to what could happen before the telephone ringing interrupted his train of thought.

Todd was very surprised to hear Mark's voice on the line, as this was the last thing that he had expected. Likewise, he was surprised that Mark made no reference to the kiss. He only asked Todd if he was going to the cinema later that evening with some more of their friends. This left him not knowing what was going to happen. Todd was in a state of apprehension and wished there was someone with whom he could confide his secret to and ask for their advice. But there wasn't anyone. His secret only had him for company.

The outing to the cinema was pleasant and enjoyable. After the film was over Todd observed Mark whilst he spoke to the group about his fears of going to court the following week – and how angry his parents were at him that they had decided not to take time off work to accompany him to court.

'I'll go with you,' piped up Todd.

'Will you?' replied Mark – in a tone of voice suggesting surprise – yet containing delight at the kind suggestion.

The evening ended with Todd making arrangements with Mark where to meet up on Monday. He then walked home by himself feeling happy that it would be him that would be helping Mark and not anyone else.

Todd was fully aware that dreams never seem real or possible unless you play an important part in them. His dreams of Mark had not yet come full circle. Todd thought about all the possibilities that might happen between Mark and himself. Mark might tell him that he was glad that he had kissed him. Mark might even kiss him back or even tell him that he loved him. Then they could make all sorts of plans for the future. Of course, they would have to discuss ways of keeping their love affair secret.

But then Todd's thoughts turned to more negative images. What if Mark took pity on him and made out that he had a problem? Maybe Mark might just tell him that he wasn't interested, that he was straight but would remain friends with him. Worst of all in Todd's mind was the fear that Mark might be gay but that he did not actually fancy him.

And for now there was nothing that he could do for the next few days except to mull over the endless possibilities. Then another thought came into his mind before he went to sleep. What if the judge took a harsh view of Mark stealing the watch and decided to punish him by sending him to a young offenders' institute. If that happened he decided he would make sure that he would visit Mark twice weekly. He was too tired to think any more about it. He said to himself before falling asleep, '*Roll on Monday*'.

Todd met Mark at the bus stop before travelling to court, which was a seven-mile journey away. Neither of them spoke very much – except for Mark who focused the conversation on how angry his parents were with him. Todd sensed how anxious Mark was feeling.

'Thanks for coming today,' Mark said in a low voice to Todd.

'No problem. I hope you don't go to jail,' replied Todd before realising that this was the wrong thing to have said.

Mark need not have worried too much though about prison. Whilst he did get a bit of a ticking off from the magistrates for stealing the watch, he escaped a prison sentence. He was simply overjoyed but had forgotten the name of the punishment he was given. All he could recall was that a social worker would be calling to his home to visit him every fortnight.

Todd was delighted too that Mark wasn't imprisoned. 'Fantastic news,' he exclaimed.

'You're telling me – I was scared shitless that I was going to get banged up,' Mark replied before leaning over to give a bear hug to Todd. As he did this Todd felt a tight squeeze in his back. As this was happening Mark announced to Todd, 'You are my best friend in the world.'

Todd was speechless with delight upon hearing these words. He didn't know how to reply but clumsily suggested instead that they should go and get some ice cream.

It was a beautiful sunny and windy afternoon. They sat on a bench eating the ice cream whilst watching the town river. It was a majestic sight with the swift current of the river flowing freely downstream. Love at that given moment was everything that it should be – exhilarating, powerful, and sincere.

Ursula

Screams, laughter and anticipation were all rolled into one. Ursula had just got stuck on a wire crossing the fence as she rushed to the circus with her friend. She had stolen the tickets for the matinee performance. She justified the theft by saying that she had a 'bit of a cash flow' problem. Not that she ever had much money but her reputation in recent weeks had grown as a result of the credit card she'd suddenly acquired.

It wasn't a love of circuses that prompted Ursula to go to this particular event. She had become intrigued about one of the trapeze artists called Ricardo who was performing in the show. Ursula had heard claims that he had a fantastic physique and was basically 'a bit of a hunk'. She set her mind on seeing him and if she considered that he was half as gorgeous as the claims made him out to be, she didn't rule out chatting him up afterwards. But for the moment she was going nowhere as she tried to untangle her crotch from the wire on the fence.

'These jeans cost me a fortune,' Ursula said to her friend, fearful that she might rip them.

'I don't know why we didn't just use the front entrance like everyone else… we still have to show them the tickets to get in,' Ursula's friend replied.

'Chill,' Ursula said, finally freeing herself.

Not only were Ursula's jeans new, so too were the other clothes she was wearing. It all happened by accident when she opened the letter addressed to her mother. She decided that a credit card would come in very useful for getting new clothes.

'The launch of Ursula's summer wardrobe is coming your way soon,' she announced to her friends upon telling them of her scam.

Even though, at that stage, she had only just posted the application off, she claimed to her friends her certainty that the credit card company would believe her lie on the application form that she was a probation officer. Ursula told her friends that it was best to pick a profession that wasn't 'bent'. After all probation officers wouldn't tell lies, she concluded. And sure enough her trick worked and the credit card arrived three weeks later with a handsome credit limit. Her parents were out when it arrived and so its arrival went unnoticed. Ursula filled her time with lots of shopping. She bought lots and lots of new clothes, the best make-up and several pairs of shoes. It was all within her grasp and grasp it she did, until she reached the credit limit on the card.

Ursula knew many probation officers. In fact she often joked that she saw more of them than she did her real parents. This was because her parents were seldom both out of prison at the same time. Their offences relating to drugs and petty theft meant they were almost alternately in prison. In between, life for Ursula meant that she was fully introduced to the cycle of care proceedings that entailed endless interviews with various support agencies. Afterwards she would be asked to pack her belongings before being sent to stay with either relatives or foster carers. At least now she thought if she had to pack in a hurry, she would have nice clothes to put in her bags.

But things had now settled down for the past two years. Ursula's parents had begun to turn over a new leaf and were getting into less trouble. However, she found herself following their previous bad habits – but was now beginning to think that perhaps obtaining the credit card hadn't been such a good idea after all, despite the initial thrill of a trendy new wardrobe. But for now she was at the circus to see her 'hunk' and right at that moment that was all that mattered.

The music was loud and had a fast rhythm to it. The act consisted of two little Chinese dolls joined together dancing at a furious speed across the ring. Ursula found the act amusing and irritating at the same time. She thought that there were two kids inside the costumes. But there was something that didn't make sense about the act. She was expecting that something would happen during the act that would be a surprise but nothing out of the ordinary happened. It just went on and on and then it suddenly stopped. Ursula's friend too thought that there were two children inside the costumes. But in actual fact what was remarkable about the act was that it was an adult inside the costumes who had the ability to curl up and pretend to be two children dancing. Out sprang a bare-chested male who took a bow from the audience.

'That's him,' screamed her friend.

'What are you talking about? Yuck, it can't be. He's an ugly git, he is,' replied Ursula with a strong hint of disappointment in her voice.

Ursula's friend said he fitted the description their friends had given them.

'Well, I think he's gorgeous,' her friend went on to say – before adding, 'He's really sexy.'

'If you think that, you're welcome to him. Did you see how smooth his chest was? How can you fancy a man who waxes his chest? Yuck,' Ursula replied.

Ursula's disappointment was soon replaced when she became completely transfixed by the next act. She thought what she was seeing was utterly stunning. The grace, skill and precision of the female trapeze artist had her completely mesmerised. The artist wasn't much older than Ursula and looked very much like a ballerina. Ursula had dreamed of becoming a dancer when she was younger. Momentary envy flashed across her mind but this soon passed as she concentrated on the movements. The trapeze artist used her hands to walk down a stepladder while her legs were evenly spread out at the same time. Not a flicker of movement took place in her legs as she did this. Ursula considered that it was the most amazing thing she had ever seen.

In spite of Ursula not sharing her friend's lust for Ricardo, she was enjoying herself and was glad that she had come. It had succeeded in getting her mind off the burden she was carrying around. The terror of being found out and the repercussions of this weighed heavily on her thoughts. Ursula put on a good act that most people accepted. The clothes, the credit card and the bravado were a mask on what she was feeling inside. She was terrified that her parents, particularly her mother whose personal details she had used to get the credit card, would get into serious trouble. When her mother remarked to her about the new clothes she was wearing, Ursula made the excuse that she had borrowed them from a friend. Ursula feared that the credit card company wouldn't believe her mother because of her criminal record and would report the matter to the police. She knew she would face fierce arguments with her mother after the truth was revealed. All of this would unsettle things at home, especially since she had been getting on really well with her parents in recent months.

The ringmaster announced the final act of the evening. Ursula covered her eyes in mock horror when she saw who was going to perform in this.

'Oh, look who it is, Ursula,' piped up her friend.

'Never, I don't believe it... It's that lovely man again! Can you wake me up after he's finished?' replied Ursula before continuing, 'You should see your face. You don't really fancy him, do you? He's horrible. Look at his chest. Has he put oil on it, or what?'

The final act contained swift bungee jumps. The man abseiled with precision across the ring and at the same time kept in perfect time to the music. His strength and fitness shone throughout his act. Ursula became absolutely engrossed in the gracefulness of the act as she watched him continue to abseil from one point of the ring to the ceiling with incredible swiftness and then back again. He made it look so easy to do, but it was apparent that years of training had gone into his performance. During these last few minutes of the show all worries about the credit card fraud left her thoughts.

Ursula was later to admit that, whilst the circus artist was no hunk in her eyes, his grand finale was simply sensational. It had been so good that if it hadn't been the final performance of the show she said she would have 'nicked' another few tickets and gone to see the ending again.

The circus had ended and so, too, were any preconceived fantasies about Ricardo. Now it was time for Ursula to return to the real world where she had to face the dreaded credit card bill. She was undecided about what she would do. She repeatedly went over the options in her mind. Her mother would be livid if she told her the truth so the only alternative was to either hide or destroy the bill. This would buy her some time. More time would enable her to do the thinking and plotting that was required to successfully cover her tracks.

Ursula wondered and joked to herself about the possibility of there being a credit card that would buy time – and that if such a card existed, she would have liked to have got her hands on one. More time would mean more days free from facing the wrath of her parents before they discovered her new-found expensive tastes. But there was no more time now. Reality was already upon her and there was no-one there to save her – and no abseil or any other means of escape available to free her from her dilemma.

Vince

Vince was ever so pleased to get his hands on ketamine, despite disbelieving Moss, the gang leader, who claimed that he had broken into the local veterinary practice. It was common knowledge that the building was guarded by tight security measures. However, Vince knew when to keep his mouth shut. Besides, he did not dare upset Moss, who had a reputation for easily losing his temper. Vince took a back-seat position in the group and didn't challenge what had been said.

Vince's group of friends liked to be known as the 'T' gang. This was because the letter 'T' represented a cross to them, or at least it did to Moss, and this emblem was favoured because it represented death. In addition, the gang adopted the motto 'mess with us and you'll get sorted'. For any person who stood up to the gang, the retaliation was a stabbing or heavy beating.

There was a little rap song that they sang before and after such encounters:

Check it; check it, 1, 2, 3…bang!
We're out to get 'cha for messin wit da T gang,
Quiver, shiver,
Scream if ya like
There's no-one out
To hear ya shout,
You dissed us, we listed ya,
We are scorned, you have been warned.

Vince found this hilariously funny, or at least he pretended so, when he was in the presence of Moss. He found being a member of the gang to have its advantages. He was in no doubt about this as he held the tiny packet containing ketamine in his hand. Vince was completely ill-informed about the drug but had heard Moss refer to it by the nickname 'kit kat', and was under the impression that it was excellent for enhancing sexual prowess.

'Just one drop of this and you will have the shag of your life,' Moss told Vince.

Vince was shy and sexually inexperienced and believed Moss. Therefore, he decided to put the drug to the test at the first available opportunity. He didn't have to wait long before this happened. Moss invited Vince and the other gang members to a party at his flat and promised his 'boys' that there would be lots of girls there. Vince was quieter than usual at the party. He barely spoke because he wasn't very good at making small conversation with strangers. This turned out to be a good thing as it got him noticed by a really attractive girl, who kept smiling at him before she introduced herself as Melissa.

Although Vince was actually quite good looking, he couldn't believe his luck when he saw that someone so gorgeous as Melissa was interested in him. They got on really well and it turned out, they liked the same types of music. Vince liked the fact that she was different from other girls at the party, lacking their noisy and loutish mannerisms. He thought that he had found himself a very sophisticated young lady in Melissa. Eventually, he mustered up enough courage to invite her back to his parents' house. Vince knew that nobody would be at home. With his father working nights and his mother away, he knew they'd have the place to themselves.

Vince got some of his father's lager out of the fridge and settled down on the sofa looking forward to having a very enjoyable time. They really gelled as they laughed, joked, played music and compared mobile phones. Vince had a massive DVD collection and chose several of his favourite film excerpts to show Melissa.

It was only when Melissa was in the bathroom and Vince was pouring more drinks that he remembered the ketamine. He got it out from his pocket and held it in his hand for a moment or so. Suddenly he got the notion to empty the sachet into Melissa's drink and stir it. Vince carried on as normal when Melissa returned to the room. They snuggled up to each other on the sofa and kissed. Vince watched as Melissa sipped her drink as he stroked her hair.

'Have you ever done it?' Vince suddenly blurted out.

'Done what?' replied Melissa in a jesting tone that implied she didn't know what he was talking about.

They both laughed and carried on talking about various things. Melissa complained about feeling really tired as she rested her head against Vince's chest. That was the last thing she was able to clearly remember. She then kept falling asleep and waking up. Every muscle in her body felt as if it had seized up, rendering her unable to move or speak. Her waking moments were only fleeting whilst the drug continued to take effect and eventually she fell into a deep sleep.

Vince carried Melissa into his bedroom and laid her on his bed. The excitement of undressing her aroused him and prompted him to become completely transfixed on having sex. He was a young man with a mission – a dreadfully cruel mission that he felt he had to hurriedly carry out without delay, as he feared Melissa would wake up and realise what was happening. Then without further thought Vince quickly undressed himself and then raped Melissa.

The next morning Vince was sitting at the end of the bed watching Melissa sleeping. His insensitivity was such that he was considering having sex with her again but Melissa waking up prevented this. Vince remained impervious to her distress when she realised that she was naked under the duvet. He was equally unaware that the after-effects of the drug had left her with a nauseous feeling.

'What happened?... What did you do to me?' Melissa asked.

'Nothing,' replied Vince. 'Nothing... Nothing at all... I swear.' He continued in a tone of voice that suggested he was surprised that she was asking him these questions.

Vince told her that they had both had a lot to drink and that she had decided to stop over. Melissa did not believe him but the fear of facing her mother, whom she knew would be angry with her for staying out overnight, overrode everything he was saying to her. After they had dressed Vince sneaked her out of the house because he did not want his father to see her. Whispering to her that he would ring were the last words he said before gently closing the door.

Vince tried ringing Melissa's mobile several times that day but found it always switched to voicemail. He left several messages but she never returned his calls. He shrugged this off and after a while gave it no more thought. However, the time was about to come when he would be forced to reconsider. In fact, that night was to become a night that would haunt him for the rest of his life. It was to be the beginning of a nightmare, but little did he know that it had already begun for Melissa the previous night, when he had put ketamine in her drink before raping her.

The police came to his house and arrested Vince on suspicion of raping Melissa. His father was asked to accompany him to the police station. The shame of what he had done was beginning to engulf his thoughts. He couldn't handle his thoughts as he now realised he was guilty of having done something seriously wrong.

'I didn't do it... I swear to you, I didn't do it,' he pleaded to his father, hoping that it would break the silence between them.

Vince's protestations to his father were an attempt to elicit a response from him. But it didn't work and his pleas were met with further silence. He knew his father doubted him from the look in his eyes. The realisation of what the shame would do to his family if he told the truth to the police was too unbearable to contemplate.

A plan of action was needed fast. Vince decided that he would deny everything at the police interview. He reasoned that they would believe him when he told them that Melissa had agreed to have sex with him – especially since they were both drinking beforehand. Then the ketamine crossed his mind. What if this had showed up in Melissa's blood test? Vince decided that if the police asked him questions about this, he would make up a story and tell them that Melissa had taken away some alcohol from the party and that this must have been spiked.

Despite composing lies for the police Vince was still fidgety and his palms were sweaty. An ordeal lay ahead of him as he waited to be taken into the interviewing suite. He could never be the same person again whether the police believed his lies or not. Vince had felt no pity for the trauma he put Melissa through and now he was trapped in a hellish situation himself. His future was indeed bleak and until he was ready to tell the truth it would remain so.

Wayne

It was a busy Friday morning at the clinic. Wayne walked in whilst smoking a cigarette, oblivious to the fact that smoking was not permitted inside the building. The receptionist promptly told him to extinguish it. He was none too happy at being reprimanded in such a way and sighed deeply as he extinguished the cigarette. He sat down sulkily and pretended he was reading a magazine.

Wayne glanced at the posters on the walls advertising the importance of safe sex and the dangers of contracting HIV or hepatitis. Sitting next to him was a young woman with whom he attempted to make conversation. Wayne had an assuming nature and knew that people found him attractive. With his head recently shaven he thought he looked particularly sexy. He asked the young woman why she had come to the clinic but was none too pleased when she told him to mind his own business. Sighing and looking away, his mood began to dive yet again.

Wayne had just finished a casual affair with a younger teenager. He never had any intention of dating the girl as he considered her background to be inferior to his. Nevertheless he found her attractive and reasonably intelligent. The fact that she was willing to have regular sex with him was a bonus and this meant he carried on seeing her for longer than he usually would in these circumstances. But Wayne was furious when he found out that she was seeing someone else behind his back. When he discovered she was having sex with someone else, he flew into a rage. He told her that she was nothing but a 'slut' and unworthy of his company. He felt a compulsion to hit her but restrained himself. It did not end there though. Wayne became paranoid about possible sexually-transmitted diseases he may have caught from the girl and imagined that his urine was a darker colour than usual – hence the urgent need to get himself examined.

Wayne was a little surprised when the nurse told him that the doctor didn't think that he had caught any sexually transmitted disease but would have to wait for the test results to be certain. Wayne had told the doctor that he had sex frequently and never used 'rubbers'. The doctor attempted to explain the dangers of not using condoms but Wayne wasn't remotely interested in the information. He took great pride talking about his sexual experiences and was convinced that he was the most sexually experienced amongst his peers, despite their bragging to the contrary.

Wayne thought anal sex was a gay thing so he had never tried it, but on the other hand had not dismissed the idea entirely. He had read that some blokes, who were not 'queers', had experimented with women and actually enjoyed it. Wayne was certainly someone who had the tenacity to be upfront about his liaisons but even he often jokingly admitted that he could never imagine himself having enough courage to ask a 'chick' to turn over for sex.

Wayne walked out of the clinic and lit another cigarette, his seventh that morning and it was not yet midday. It was half term from school and despite having plenty of pocket money he was bored and had nothing to do. He decided to go into town and catch up with some people he knew. Wayne didn't make friends easily or remain friends with anyone for very long either because he had adopted such an air of being superior to others – to the extent that it had consumed his personality.

Wayne's parents owned a chain of betting shops and off licences. He lived with his parents in a nice house in a quiet part on the outskirts of a town. He saw very little of them during the week. They rarely ate meals together and conversation was sparse at the best of times. Sitting listening to his father abuse his mother and make allegations of her having affairs had become a regular occurrence in his life. Sometimes not knowing what to say or do he would just sit waiting for the bickering to stop. On the occasions he tried to intervene his father would tell him to 'butt out'.

Although Wayne went away on foreign holidays with his parents every year, they seldom spent any real time together. Even on holiday, Wayne would be given money to go off and do his own thing. He didn't mind doing this as it got him away from their arguments.

Wayne knew that his father didn't trust his mother and had hired private detectives to check into her background. He often eavesdropped on his father's telephone conversations as well as opening mail that he thought would contain confidential information. He had become unstuck though when he was caught playing sleuth. His father discovered a private letter of his opened and left lying around in the living room. Wayne's father lost his temper and gave him several punches for opening his mail without permission, threatening him that if he ever interfered in his business again, he would live to regret it.

On reaching the town centre, Wayne put all thoughts of the clinic out of his mind. He met up with the usual group of friends he hung out with, neither caring for, nor particularly liking any of them. Sometimes he liked the fact that a few looked up to him and were impressed that his father owned several businesses. He liked their admiration but had no respect for anyone in the group. However, Wayne found that by pretending to like them, he could encourage them into anti-social behaviour. He would, for example, goad them into breaking a shop window or, alternatively, to empty a rubbish bin and scatter its contents all over the pavement.

After the boredom of the clinic, he was in the mood for some excitement and looked for something different to do. An elderly woman was coming along the pavement pushing a trolley full of plastic bags. Thinking it would be funny, he suggested that someone from the group should go up and take a bag from her trolley. But the other young people laughed and put the suggestion back to him. Wayne felt he was left with no option but to do it himself.

One of Wayne's acquaintances knew that the elderly woman had a mental health problem and lived at a local hostel. This information did not deter Wayne one iota when he was told this. The fact that he was about to attack a vulnerable old lady and upset her greatly did not phase him in the slightest. His desire to have fun was his only priority.

Wayne took a bag from the trolley and started waving it about in the air. The others in the group looked on and with mock laughter encouraged him to take another bag. But as he was about to do so, the bag burst and the contents fell to the ground. Letters, photographs and newspaper cuttings spilt on to the pavement. This did not prevent him from taking another bag from the trolley. Neither did the screams of the elderly woman stop him from continuing with his cruelty. Wayne thought he was being genuinely funny, despite some members of the group requesting him to stop. Eventually all the bags from the trolley were on the ground. Wayne and the others then fled the scene as the woman screamed in terror at what had happened.

Wayne found himself to be in the mood for sex after his outlandish prank on the elderly woman. The only problem was that he didn't fancy anyone in the group. He felt too lazy to go somewhere else. The thought of going to a prostitute crossed his mind – as he often had fantasies of going to a high-class 'hooker'. He had seen a few really attractive prostitutes in town and thought they would be okay for one-off sex. But a fear of getting caught and his father's reaction if this happened put a stop to him approaching one. Wayne ended up not having any sex that day and eventually, he got fed up with the company of the group and decided to go home.

That evening, he closed the front door of his house and felt the usual terrible emptiness inside. His parents were not at home. This meant spending another evening alone in the house. It was during such moments of loneliness that Wayne's mask would slip. Deep down, he was depressed and dissatisfied with his life. The charade of pretending to outsiders that he had everything in life they wanted and his display of smugness and superiority was a front to the outside world. The reality of his true world hit home every time he returned of an evening to discover he had no one to talk to or be with. Even when his parents were at home, there was never a moment of harmony, with the arguments in constant flow.

It sometimes bothered Wayne that he lived life in between two horizons. He yearned to be like his peers and was envious of them having brothers and sisters and being part of what he perceived to be normal family life. But Wayne also knew that his peers craved to be like him – and, in turn, were jealous of his self-confidence, promiscuity and material blessings. But whilst both worlds met and had similarities – they remained firmly separate from one another.

Life is so much like a pack of cards and hopefully one day Wayne would come to realise this and become content with the cards that he had been dealt.

Xanthia

Xanthia thought that she could not live without drugs. Taking drugs controlled her entire life. Xanthia's father first introduced her to drugs at home. They lived on a run-down inner-city estate in Manchester that was labelled '*The Sinking Ship*'. Everyone living there had been touched by crime, poverty and addictions of one kind or another. It was a bleak place that offered little hope to those who had become entangled in its web.

Xanthia would willingly tell strangers about the various types of drugs she had taken, in order to impress them about her experiences. But on one particular day Xanthia wasn't in any mood to boast about her drug taking. She was due to meet her social worker and it had put her in a surly mood all morning. She had run out of ideas and schemes to get hold of cash without having to rob someone. Xanthia half recalled her social worker talking about college courses and grants. She hated her social worker and never really listened to her. She was not interested in rehabilitation clinics and college courses. None of her friends were much interested in these either.

Xanthia told her social worker that she wanted to clean up her act and stop taking drugs. She lied about the extent of her drug taking and said she was now looking forward to getting on a college fashion design course. All of these statements were lies. Xanthia thought the social worker would believe her and would give her money to enrol at college. It was explained to her that things did not work this way.

'Yeah but... I want to go to college next week but I have no money,' was the bland reply she repeatedly made.

It did not take long before her hatched scheme was exposed. Xanthia just sat there with a pained and cold expression on her face.

'Look at what you are doing to me... I want to go to college but you won't help me,' she repeated in a monotonous tone.

She eventually left the office and muttered 'Whatever' as she closed the door. By now, Xanthia was at her wits' end. She needed to get her hands on some heroin. Her scam at her social worker's office had failed miserably. She felt she had no other alternative but to rob some-one so that she could get her hands on some money to buy her next fix.

She chose her victim at random. A woman was coming out of a nearby pharmacy when Xanthia pounced on her and grabbed hold of her shoulder bag. Her victim relented easily without a struggle. However, Xanthia was a little disappointed to only find a small amount of money in the bag but consoled herself that it was more than she had before the mugging. Xanthia fled from the scene as quickly as possible and headed in the direction of home.

Xanthia arrived home to the usual scene. The flat was freezing cold and the fridge contained little food. The fact that there was a fridge in the flat was a miracle in itself because her father had sold off anything worth selling – and this included the television. They had just got their electricity reconnected after having been cut off for several weeks owing to non-payment.

Xanthia asked her father if he had any smack before handing over to him the money that she had got from the mugging. They weren't alone in the flat. Billy, one of her father's regular customers was also present buying his daily fix. Billy asked Xanthia where she had got the money. She told him what she had done to get it, adding 'Another day, another robbery' in a philosophical manner before settling down to take her beloved drug.

Billy then wanted to boast about his own piece of bravado and started telling Xanthia about a bank robbery that he once participated in. He said it was better than what you'd see in a James Bond movie.

'You're talking crap, man,' Xanthia told him.

'No, believe me, I'm fucking telling you the truth,' he replied.

She was correct about this. Everything Billy was saying was make-believe nonsense that had never happened. Her father had told her about Billy who was well renowned for talking nonsense about rob-beries that he was never involved in.

Xanthia began to relax after she had injected some heroin. The flat appeared warmer despite there being no heating. The stress she endured earlier in the day had gone. She was in the mood for light-hearted banter with Billy. She accepted some beer he offered her and before long they were laughing and engrossed in conversation. Xanthia didn't take him seriously when he offered a solution to their cash-flow problem by suggesting that they rob the local off licence. She just sarcastically responded to the ideas that he presented. In the meantime her father was taking his fix for the evening.

'I know where I can get my hands on a couple of balaclavas and a fake gun,' Billy told Xanthia as he slurped his drink.

Xanthia nearly choked on her drink with laughter and had to spit out what she had in her mouth.

'Fuck off, you idiot... I don't think you'd know the difference between a balaclava and a bucket of sand,' she replied back to him.

Her father too was beginning to unwind after injecting himself and began to take an interest in the discussion about the robbery. This surprised Xanthia because her father mainly relied on the income that he received through his drug dealing. The discussion continued and during the course of the evening a large quantity of alcohol was consumed. Xanthia and Billy then finalised their plans to rob the local off licence the next evening. That was the last that she remembered of the conversation before crashing out on the sofa.

The next morning she woke to the most frightening experience of her life. She discovered that Billy had died whilst sleeping next to her on the sofa. It was instantly obvious to her that he was dead because he looked so pale and grey and his mouth was wide open. There was dried blood all around his nose and mouth. Xanthia screamed and woke her father who was asleep in one of the nearby armchairs. Her father tested Billy's pulse and he confirmed to Xanthia that he was indeed dead. Then panic set in. Xanthia was so shocked that she repeatedly kept asking her father what they would do.

After a few moments of intense thinking they decided that the best thing was to get as far away from the flat as possible. Xanthia suggested going to stay with their uncle on his farm in the west of Ireland. Her father agreed that this was a good idea – and together they agreed to travel to Ireland by boat. Xanthia then packed a few belongings and reminded her father not to forget to take his supply of heroin with him and after that they hastily set out on their journey.

Xanthia waited with her father to embark on the ferry to Dublin. She knew there was going to be no turning back now. Neither was she sure of what lay ahead, but feelings of indifference overcrowded anything else in her mind at that point in time. Xanthia squirmed when she saw a police officer near the point of embarkation. She suddenly remembered that her father was carrying heroin and together they risked getting caught. She inwardly gave a huge sigh of relief when they got through without being stopped. Xanthia needed a drink and persuaded her father to go to the bar and get her a glass of wine. She knew they had to think quickly and come up with a good excuse to tell their relatives in Ireland about their unexpected arrival.

Xanthia had always wanted to visit Ireland. Destiny holds many surprises. However, going to Ireland under these circumstances was a surprise that she could have done without. But Xanthia knew that there was no other alternative for her father and herself – because there were few options available that prevented taking responsibility. Then the boat began its journey taking Xanthia away from the unremitting misery that she and her father were leaving behind – but were also taking with them.

Yuan

Yuan had few real friends. It was not that he had difficulty in making them but found sustaining friendships difficult because of the amount of trouble other young people got into by associating with him. He had just got himself out of trouble quite recently with the police. Yuan and a group of others had been caught on camera throwing stones from a fly-over onto cars passing underneath. Yuan was the main instigator in this. It started innocently enough with small little pebbles but gradually larger stones were used. Yuan loved the thrill of aiming the stones at the bonnets of cars despite the danger it caused to motorists. One or two of the cars had to swerve quickly and narrowly missed other cars travelling in the opposite direction which added to Yuan's delight.

Generally nothing interested Yuan for longer than a couple of minutes – except motorbikes. Although he was clever, he had little interest in school. Disruptive behaviour made it impossible for teachers to engage him in lessons. Pinching, nudging and shoving others made life in his presence very testing. He would walk up and down the classroom, shouting out aloud answers that were usually the first thing that had come into his head. Jumping up on the furniture and then suddenly dashing to the window every time he heard a sound outside, made it a constant battle for the teacher to gain control.

Yuan was no better at home. The only consolation was that his parents allowed him to smoke. This often helped to settle a situation when his anger was getting out of control. His father had a motorbike and this too was an enormous help in keeping him occupied. Yuan often went for a ride with his father but would complain that his father did not travel fast enough. Contact with motorbikes eventually resulted in Yuan becoming fixated with them. Little scooters did not interest him. He preferred motorbikes with high-powered engines and knew the names of every type.

'Whoopee, that's a nice cruiser,' he had a habit of saying every time he saw a different model.

Harley Davidson's were a big favourite but he rarely saw any in his area. He often said that the next time he saw one he would try and steal it but was only joking though.

Yuan could be found out in the backyard of his home most evenings. He often ran into the house and pestered his father to give him the keys so that he could go for a ride by himself. He didn't listen when his father told him that this would be dangerous as well as illegal. The keys were hidden just in case he was tempted to go for the forbidden spin by himself whilst his father's back was turned. After receiving several refusals Yuan would return to the backyard and enjoy a game of simulation on the motorbike. He did this for long periods, noisily pretending to turn corners, and then increasing speed to overtake other vehicles.

On returning indoors, his disruptive behaviour continued unabated until bedtime, and, even then, it would take a long time to settle. Tiredness seldom got the better of Yuan and he always appeared to have an enormous supply of energy. He would refuse to go to bed every night without inducement. Bribery was usually by means of cigarettes with Yuan smoking at least four or five of these before relenting to his parents' request to go to bed.

The head teacher asked the school's educational psychologist to assess Yuan. He hated the assessment and couldn't see the point answering questions that he considered boring. The questions entailed getting Yuan's perception about difficulties he was having at school, how well he got on with his classmates – and asking him details about his parents and home life. Yuan didn't participate well in the session and refused to attend subsequent appointments.

The educational psychologist eventually referred Yuan to a psychiatrist. Yuan's parents agreed to accompany him to the appointment. Yuan paced up and down in the waiting room. Anxiety for a cigarette was getting the better of him and his mother remonstrated with him to sit down. Just at that moment, they were called into the psychiatrist's office. After brief introductions the psychiatrist started flicking through the reports from the school psychologist. He briefly looked over his glasses at Yuan and his parents as he studied the paperwork. Then the psychiatrist asked Yuan about his interests.

'Well I like motorbikes – and I like girls,' replied Yuan before breaking into laughter.

'And what about school, young man, do you like school?' continued the psychiatrist.

'I suppose it's ok,' Yuan managed to reply before getting up and walking to the window. 'Dad, come and look at this – there is a cruiser outside.'

The psychiatrist got impatient and didn't ask any more questions.

'A definite case of Attention Deficit Hyperactivity Disorder,' he announced to Yuan and his parents.

'What the frig is that?' Yuan asked with a confused look on his face.

'You're having trouble with your attention, young man,' replied the psychiatrist, and added: 'You will find the tablets that I'm going to prescribe beneficial.' The psychiatrist handed over a few pamphlets containing information on the condition and then talked about the medication he was going to prescribe for Yuan.

'Hopefully these tablets will help sort things out,' he said as he was ushering Yuan and his parents out of the office.

Yuan was delighted to get out of the psychiatrist's office. He was longing for a cigarette and did not give a thought about the diagnosis of ADHD. Anyway, he didn't understand what the psychiatrist was talking about but agreed to take the medication, as this was what his parents had wanted.

But things did not work out as anticipated. The medication may have dampened his energetic ways but it made him very grumpy – he found it difficult to sleep, which meant that during the day he constantly felt tired. Then there was the diarrhoea and loss of appetite. He also lost all interest in motorbikes to the point that his father no longer had to hide the keys. All in all, the medication seemed to have transformed Yuan into an unhappy and ill teenager. Furthermore, an aggressive edge to his personality had developed which was totally out of character.

Yuan

Yuan hated mathematics at school. He had no patience with figures and often complained that he considered it a stupid subject. The maths teacher was demonstrating a new equation to the class when he noticed that Yuan had begun to fall asleep. He went over and asked Yuan to stand up and explain to everyone the equation. Yuan became embarrassed and mumbled a wrong answer. The teacher launched into a tirade of criticism about inattentive behaviour but before he could finish speaking, Yuan stormed out of the classroom screaming 'Leave me alone – stop picking on me.'

The diarrhoea and sleeplessness continued until, in the end, Yuan stopped taking the medication. He had heard that someone else at his school had stopped taking similar tablets and this encouraged him to follow suit. Yuan's parents tried to persuade him otherwise since they continued to believe the psychiatrist's prognosis that his behaviour would eventually improve. However, Yuan was adamant that he would no longer take the tablets, and pointed out to his parents that they weren't the ones being sick all the time. Fortunately and possibly unexpectedly, once he had stopped taking the medication he began sleeping better and his aggressiveness ceased. His parents noticed the improvement and relented in their protests to take further medication, which pleased him immensely.

After a few days Yuan could be heard yet again in the backyard as he played on the motorbike. Fantastic fun surrounded him as he imagined that he was overtaking a large lorry but had to do so quickly in order to avoid a sharp bend ahead. Then one evening he ran into the kitchen and blurted out in an excited tone 'I'm gonna be a mechanic,' telling his parents his plans for the future. Yuan had made up his mind that he wanted to train as a mechanic after he left school. He had it all worked out in his mind that he would be able to work with motorbikes all day long and learn how to fix their engines. There would also be the prospect of repairing old motorbikes and selling them for a handsome profit. One day he might even own his own garage and employ people to help him with the repairs. Yuan's dreams were large and bright – but were yet attainable and within his grasp.

Zane

Zane and his friend stood on the street corner and watched a young woman moving boxes from a house to a nearby car. They were judging the situation and discussed how best to approach her. The friend suggested just walking up to her and casually asking if she had a spare cigarette. Zane, himself, thought it would be better if they pretended to be lost by asking her for directions. Eventually Zane's friend grew impatient waiting and said he was going home. Zane nearly did the same but decided to wait and see what would happen.

Unbeknown to him, the woman he had been watching was Elaine Smyth who was clearing things out of her flat. She was soon getting married and was moving into a new house that she and her fiancé had just bought. It had been a stressful day for Elaine. She had hurried home from work to do some of the packing. She also felt that she had hundreds of things to do in preparation for her wedding day. She started loading the boxes in the boot of her car, oblivious that a young predator was closely watching her by the name of Zane.

Zane walked up to Elaine as she was coming out of the house with a box and pretended to ask for directions. Zane then asked her if she had a spare cigarette. Elaine told him that she did not smoke and added in a joking manner that she thought he was too young to be smoking. It was at this point that Zane started to grab the box she was holding which contained a new laptop computer.

Elaine put up a struggle and shouted for help. This annoyed Zane. He told her to 'shut up' but she continued to scream for help. His anger suddenly intensified and then he gave her a hard punch in the face. The force of the blow cut her face around her mouth. She put her hand to her face and discovered she was bleeding. However, Elaine was determined not to let him get away with it. She began shouting louder and louder. Unfortunately there was nobody else in the street at the time and her cries for help went unnoticed.

Zane was surprised and none too pleased at what was happening. He had committed several street robberies and usually his victims did not put up any resistance – especially women. Now he feared for his credibility and feared that his father would tease him for this.

'Ha ha ha, a woman got the better of you Zaneie,' he could hear his father saying in his mind.

His father always called him Zaneie. Zane liked his father styling his name this way. He lived at home with his father, in a house that was compiled of stolen goods. His father liked to think of himself as a 'career thief'. Over the past year a kind of rivalry had developed between him and Zane. This had started out as a joke but Zane took the jest a little bit too seriously and tried his best to outshine his father with the number of stolen goods he could take home, including money.

Elaine managed to tug the box away from Zane but then she tripped on the kerb and fell awkwardly onto the ground. He finally got hold of the box, but this wasn't enough for him. He was upset at being challenged and kicked Elaine whilst she lay on the ground, narrowly missing her head. He then asked Elaine if she had any money. He took her car keys and went over and unlocked the boot and started rummaging through her belongings.

Zane thought he had got the upper hand with Elaine. Whilst going through her possessions he failed to notice that she had managed to get up and had run across the road to a nearby pub. It only dawned on him that she had slipped away after he suddenly heard loud voices and saw Elaine coming towards him accompanied by two men. The men gave chase but could not catch up with Zane, as he was a faster runner than them.

Although Zane was winded from running he managed to look round and saw that the two men had stopped chasing him. He gave no thought to Elaine or how she might be feeling. There wasn't anything unusual about this because Zane rarely thought about his victims after he had robbed them. His mind was always preoccupied with plans for his next robbery, which left no room to worry about any trauma he had caused.

Zane was flushed and out of breath as he boarded the bus home. He remained angry with himself for leaving the laptop and other items behind. He wondered how he had been so stupid for not having noticed the men approaching sooner. He considered it a very unprofitable evening. Nevertheless, he reassured himself 'Never mind Zaneie, you will have better luck tomorrow'. Zane, of course, could never visualise that his 'tomorrows' would eventually run out of luck and that he would be caught. Thoughts of him facing up to the reality of his actions were far from his mind. He sat on the bus and began to make up an impressive story about the evening to tell his father.

The thought of disappointing his father was greater than the anger he held towards himself for the bungled robbery. But the greatest shame for Zane was the prospect of being perceived as a failure in his father's eyes. He knew he would not be able to cope if his father referred to him as being weak – and decided he would have to conceal what had really happened that evening and invent a story around it.

When he got home his father asked him how profitable his evening had been. Zane responded to the question by giving a dramatised account of the failed robbery, exaggerating parts of it here and there, in an attempt to amuse his father.

'You're still not as clever as your old man,' exclaimed his father holding up a collection of gold chains that he had stolen that evening.

'Fucking hell, how did you get your hands on them dad?' Zane asked.

Then they spent the rest of the evening discussing how they would sell the gold chains and how much money they could generate. The whole conversation between Zane and his father contained bravado with each of them pretending to be more courageous than the other. They began to discuss how they would sell the chains. Plans for this were interspersed with ideas for another haul that would supposedly earn them even more capital.

But nothing was fully decided before bedtime. They would resume the discussion next morning. They often did this. There was something about discussing robberies at the breakfast table that added excitement to the rest of the day. Subconsciously, they had discovered that the missing void in their relationship was best filled in this way.

The End

Acknowledgements

Writing a book can be a lonely and solitary task. In fact no writer can afford the luxury of being an island unto themselves. A small army of helpers in the background assist and guide the process until the final draft reaches fruition. *Glimpses* is no exception to this rule and therefore I would like to thank the following people who have helped me live my dream of being recognised as a writer.

I would like to make special mention of my editorial team – Patricia Hardwicke and Marie Holdaway for their patience, dedication and hard work.

To Simon Kelly at The London Press who has been extremely helpful and pleasant to work with – and to Penny Purchase for her artistic design of the jacket cover.

Special recognition to my dear friend and psychologist – Sofia Chrysou who provided psychological advice and debate on the text and characters in *Glimpses*. Sofia and I seldom agreed on anything. My views of personality disorder and the damaged psyche clashed with her views on the complexities of human nature. But we shared excellent camaraderie in our conflict and differing views. Sofia has left a void in my life since she returned to live in Greece.

A big thank you to my sponsor – Bluecare Social Care in London – especially Cynthia Downs. Cynthia's advice and knowledge as a former editor in the publishing industry was much appreciated. I would also like to thank Greg McKague and Frances Newman for their help with marketing and promotion.

I would like to extend thanks to the esteemed artist Hayley McAuley for her assistance with the lyrics contained in the stories – Vince and Olga.

A note of thanks to my friend Elizabeth Hill for her spiritual advice on the lives of the characters in *Glimpses*. Elizabeth's intuition and insight into human nature is simply fascinating. It is such a privilege to know Elizabeth and to count her among my friends.

And, last but not least, my book would not be complete without mentioning my social work friends – Helen Vassie, of Sittingbourne Youth Offending Team and Verity Bradley, of Rochester Community Mental Health Team. I thank them both for their valued social work advice.

Author's Profile

Declan Henry is a qualified social worker who has been working in the profession since 1993. He is a postgraduate from King's College, London where he attained a Master of Science Degree in Mental Health Social Work.

Declan began his social work career doing voluntary work with Centrepoint in London, working with young, homeless people – many of whom suffered drug, alcohol and mental health problems.

Declan worked for four years at senior level in forensic mental health in London, working with mentally disordered offenders – many of whom had severe personality disorders and committed very significant crimes including murder and serious sexual offences. More recently, he has worked with persistent young offenders. The children he has worked with were considered to be the most wayward and dangerously disturbed children in the UK.

Declan is a prolific writer and has written several short stories and articles. He has also written *'Buried Deep in my Heart'* – his childhood autobiography – to be published in due course. He has also previously contributed to academic and research publications as well as allowing some of his material to be used in writing workshops in Ireland.